The *European Union*

Political, Social, and Economic Cooperation

EUROPEAN UNION

POLITICAL, SOCIAL, AND ECONOMIC COOPERATION

The European Union

Political, Social, and Economic Cooperation

FRANCE

by
Jeanine Sanna

Mason Crest Publishers
Philadelphia

Mason Crest Publishers Inc.
370 Reed Road, Broomall, Pennsylvania 19008
(866) MCP-BOOK (toll free)
www.masoncrest.com

First printing
1 2 3 4 5 6 7 8 9 10

Library of Congress Cataloging-in-Publication Data

Sanna, Jeanine.
   France / by Jeanine Sanna.
      p. cm.—(The European Union)
   Includes index.
      ISBN 1-4222-0047-7
      ISBN 1-4222-0038-8 (series)
   1. France—Juvenile literature. 2. European Union—France—Juvenile literature. I. Title. II. European Union (Series) (Philadelphia, Pa.)
   DC17.S28 2006
   944—dc22
                                        2005022616

Produced by Harding House Publishing Service, Inc.
www.hardinghousepages.com
Interior design by Benjamin Stewart.
Cover design by MK Bassett-Harvey.
Printed in the Hashemite Kingdom of Jordan.

CONTENTS

THE
EUROPEAN
UNION

GREENLAND SEA

ICELAND
★ Reykjavík

NORWEGIAN SEA

BARENTS SEA

RUSSIA

White Sea

FINLAND
Tampere ●
Turku ●
Helsinki ◉

Oulu ●

Bergen ●
Lillehammer ●
Frederikstad ●
NORWAY
Oslo ◉

SWEDEN
Gothenburg ●
Norrköping ●
Stockholm ◉

Gulf of Bothnia

Kristiansund ●

ESTONIA
Tallinn ★
Tartu ●

Gulf of Finland

LATVIA
Ventspils ●
Riga ★
Daugavpils ●

Gulf of Riga

★ Moscow

DENMARK
Aalborg ●
Helsingborg ●
Odense ●
Copenhagen ◉
Malmö ●

Skagerrak
Kattegat

BALTIC SEA

LITHUANIA
Klaipėda ●
Kaunas ●
Vilnius ◉

RUSSIA

BELARUS
★ Minsk

UNITED KINGDOM
Glasgow ●
Edinburgh ●
Belfast ●

NORTH SEA

Hamburg ●
Gdańsk ●

IRELAND
Dublin ◉
Killarney ●
Cork ●

Irish Sea

Liverpool ●
Manchester ●
Birmingham ●
London ●

St George's Channel

English Channel

THE NETHERLANDS
The Hague ●
Rotterdam ● Amsterdam ◉

Berlin ◉
Leipzig ●

POLAND
Warsaw ◉
Wrocław ●

BELGIUM
Brussels ◉
LUXEMBOURG
Luxembourg ◉

Düsseldorf ●
Cologne ●
GERMANY
Frankfurt am Main ●
Stuttgart ●

Dresden ●

Kraków ●

UKRAINE
Kyiv ★

Paris ◉

Nantes ●

FRANCE

Plzeň ●
Prague ●
Brno ●
CZECH REPUBLIC
Košice ●
SLOVAKIA
Bratislava ●
Győr ●

Munich ●
Linz ●
Salzburg ●
Vienna ●

MOLDOVA
Chișinău ★

Sea of Azov

Bern ◉
SWITZERLAND
AUSTRIA
HUNGARY
Budapest ◉
Szeged ●

ROMANIA
Bucharest ★

Lyons ●
Bordeaux ●

Ljubljana ★
Zagreb ★
Trieste ●
Venice ●
SLOVENIA
CROATIA
BOSNIA-HERCEGOVINA
Sarajevo ●

Belgrade ★
YUGOSLAVIA

Sofia ★
BULGARIA

BLACK SEA

Bay of Biscay

Milan ●
Turin ●

Toulouse ●
Marseille ●
Nice ●

Florence ●

Gulf de Lion

Vigo ●
Porto ●
Bilbao ●

PORTUGAL
Lisbon ◉

SPAIN
Madrid ●
Valencia ●
Barcelona ●

Faro ●
Seville ●

Strait of Gibraltar

ITALY
Rome ●

Naples ●

TYRRHENIAN SEA

ADRIATIC SEA

Skopje ★
MACEDONIA

ALBANIA

Thessaloniki ●

AEGEAN SEA

GREECE
Kalamata ●
Athens ◉

IONIAN SEA

Ankara ★
TURKEY

Lefkosia (Nicosia) ★
CYPRUS
Lemessos ●

LEBANON

MEDITERRANEAN SEA

Sea of Crete

MALTA
Valetta ●

MEDITERRANEAN SEA

Algiers ★
Tunis ★

Rabat ●

MOROCCO

ALGERIA

TUNISIA

Tripoli ★

LIBYA

ISRAEL & THE PALESTINIAN TERRITORIES

Cairo ★

EGYPT

FRANCE

European Union Member since 1952

Lille

Amiens

Rouen

Caen

Reims

Metz

Nancy

Brest

★ **Paris**

Versailles

Strasbourg

Rennes

Le Mans

Orléans

Nantes

Tours

Dijon

Limoges

Lyon

Clermont-Ferrand

St-Etienne

Grenoble

Bordeaux

Monaco

Nimes

Nice

Toulouse

Montpellier

Marseille

INTRODUCTION

Sixty years ago, Europe lay scarred from the battles of the Second World War. During the next several years, a plan began to take shape that would unite the countries of the European continent so that future wars would be inconceivable. On May 9, 1950, French Foreign Minister Robert Schuman issued a declaration calling on France, Germany, and other European countries to pool together their coal and steel production as "the first concrete foundation of a European federation." "Europe Day" is celebrated each year on May 9 to commemorate the beginning of the European Union (EU).

The EU consists of twenty-five countries, spanning the continent from Ireland in the west to the border of Russia in the east. Eight of the ten most recently admitted EU member states are former communist regimes that were behind the Iron Curtain for most of the latter half of the twentieth century.

Any European country with a democratic government, a functioning market economy, respect for fundamental rights, and a government capable of implementing EU laws and policies may apply for membership. Bulgaria and Romania are set to join the EU in 2007. Croatia and Turkey have also embarked on the road to EU membership.

While the EU began as an idea to ensure peace in Europe through interconnected economies, it has evolved into so much more today:

- Citizens can travel freely throughout most of the EU without carrying a passport and without stopping for border checks.

- EU citizens can live, work, study, and retire in another EU country if they wish.

- The euro, the single currency accepted throughout twelve of the EU countries (with more to come), is one of the EU's most tangible achievements, facilitating commerce and making possible a single financial market that benefits both individuals and businesses.

- The EU ensures cooperation in the fight against cross-border crime and terrorism.

- The EU is spearheading world efforts to preserve the environment.

- As the world's largest trading bloc, the EU uses its influence to promote fair rules for world trade, ensuring that globalization also benefits the poorest countries.

- The EU is already the world's largest donor of humanitarian aid and development assistance, providing 55 percent of global official development assistance to developing countries in 2004.

The EU is neither a nation intended to replace existing nations, nor an international organization. The EU is unique—its member countries have established common institutions to which they delegate some of their sovereignty so that decisions on matters of joint interest can be made democratically at the European level.

Europe is a continent with many different traditions and languages, but with shared values such as democracy, freedom, and social justice, cherished values well known to North Americans. Indeed, the EU motto is "United in Diversity."

Enjoy your reading. Take advantage of this chance to learn more about Europe and the EU!

Ambassador John Bruton,
Head of Delegation of the European Commission, Washington, D.C.

France's rugged landscape

CHAPTER 1

THE LANDSCAPE

*B*ienvenue à France! In other words, welcome to France. The largest country in Western Europe, France is a place where the old and the new exist together; ancient Roman ruins can be seen right next to modern-day houses, and medieval towns are just minutes away from bustling urban centers. Breathtakingly beautiful, France is—and has been for centuries—a popular tourist destination.

GEOGRAPHY

France's geography is incredibly varied. To the south and central regions are hills, while plains and lowlands form the northern area. Then there are the Alps to the east and the Pyrenees to the south. These huge mountains form equally impressive valleys filled with all kinds of plant and animal life. The Alps are a natural boundary passable only by taking narrow zigzagging roads up and down the mountains. Driving on these almost too-narrow roads, a tourist may marvel as the natives zoom up and down at impressive speed, seeming to show no concern for the fact that the car is hundreds of feet in the air and that there is no guardrail, or even shoulder, protecting the unwary from falling to the valley below.

FRANCE'S NEIGHBORS

Around twice the size of Colorado, France has an area of 211,209 square miles (547,030 square kilometers). While the country is bordered to the west, northwest, and southeast by water, France has many neighboring countries as well. These include Belgium, Luxembourg, Germany, Switzerland, Monaco, and Italy to the north and east as well as Spain and Andorra to the south.

It is a short distance across the English Channel (*La Manche*, or the Sleeve, in French) to England, and many tourists travel the Chunnel (the tunnel that spans the English Channel) in both directions. While in France, it is not uncommon to see a car with the driver on the right-hand side, even in the southernmost parts of the country.

THE CLIMATE

Because of the wind that blows off the Atlantic Ocean, bringing warm temperatures with it, France has a relatively moderate climate. This results in mild winters and cool summers, with temperatures in the French capital of Paris rarely getting below 34° to 40°F (1° to 6°C) in the winter or above 55° to 75°F (13° to 24°C) in the summer. While this proximity to the sea means a warmer climate, the winds that travel through France also bring precipitation. Because of this, it is not uncommon for skies to be overcast and for a steady drizzle to fall from the clouds. However, the temperature rarely gets cold enough to snow.

Though this oceanic climate applies to most of central France, in the northeastern areas, the weather is affected more by winds coming from over the land. This **continental** climate results in cold winters and hot summers. Snowstorms are not uncommon in this part of the country and in cities like Strasbourg. Once winter is over, frequent thunderstorms bring heavy precipitation as temperatures rise and summer comes.

A third climate, which affects mainly southern France, is the Mediterranean climate. This results in a much warmer climate than in the rest of France, with mild, wet winters and hot, dryer summers. Mistrals, cool, dry winds that blow from the north, can sometimes bring cooler weather during the winters, but for the most part, the temperature stays between 35° and 50°F (2° to 10°C) even in the coldest months. The summers are another story, with temperatures reaching

A backbone of red rock crosses Southern France.

84°F (29°C). This climate also affects the island of Corsica, considered to be a part of France.

In the mountains like the Alps and the Pyrenees, a few areas stay snowy all year long. Many ski resorts have been built there and are popular tourist destinations. While these climates are much more severe than what is found in the rest of France, they are not widespread, contained to the more mountainous areas.

CHAPTER ONE—THE LANDSCAPE

WATERWAYS

France has many important rivers. One of these, the Seine, flows into the Atlantic Ocean and provides a water route to and from the city of Paris. Another river, the Loire, is the longest river in France. Because its water level changes often, floods are not uncommon.

While both of these rivers are entirely in France, other bodies of water run through the country as well. One of these, the River Rhône, travels from Switzerland to the Mediterranean Sea, and is the largest river in France. The Rhine also originates from the Swiss Alps, then goes through Germany and the Netherlands to the North Sea.

A network of canals connects all France's waterways, most of which are navigable. There are not many lakes, but one, Lake Geneva, is on the border between France and Switzerland.

FAUNA AND FLORA

France has been settled for centuries, long before Europeans ever set foot on North America. Because of this, many of the ***indigenous*** species that once inhabited the land have become extinct through human interference. However, the country has made efforts in recent years to conserve the remaining wilderness.

Vegetation varies with the different climates, which often may depend on the elevation. At the top of the mountains, barely below

---

QUICK FACTS: THE GEOGRAPHY OF FRANCE

Location: Western Europe, bordering the Bay of Biscay and the English Channel, between Belgium and Spain; bordering the Mediterranean Sea between Italy and Spain.

Area: slightly smaller than twice the size of Colorado
  total: 211,209 square miles (547,030 sq. km.)
  land: 210,669 square miles (545,630 sq. km.)
  water: 541 square miles (1,400 sq. km.)

Borders: Andorra 35 miles (57 km.), Belgium 385 miles (620 km.), Germany 280 miles (451 km.), Italy 303 miles (488 km.), Luxembourg 45 miles (73 km.), Monaco 3 miles (4 km.), Spain 387 miles (623 km.), Switzerland 356 miles (573 km.)

Climate: cool winters and mild summers, but mild winters and hot summers along the Mediterranean; occasional strong, cold, dry, north-to-northwesterly wind known as mistral

Terrain: mostly flat plains or gently rolling hills in the north and west; mountainous elsewhere, Pyrenees in the south and the Alps in the east

Elevation extremes:
  lowest point: Rhone River delta— –7feet (–2 meters)
  highest point: Mont Blanc—15,771 feet (4,807 meters)

Natural hazards: flooding, avalanches, midwinter windstorms, drought, forest fires in the south

Source: www.cia.gov, 2005.

---

the snow line, the only plant life is lichens and mosses, clinging tenaciously to the more sheltered rocks. As one descends, alpine pastures become visible. Here, sheep and goats graze during the warmer months.

After the fields in the timberline, a **coniferous** forest grows up. Trees like fir, larch, and spruce can be found here. At the bottom of the mountain is a ***deciduous*** forest. Once covering most of the lower mountains and plains, this forest is now restricted to very limited areas, the land once filled with oak and chestnut trees now used for farmland.

Evidence of ancient human settlement is also evident in the Mediterranean area. What was once covered in various types of vegetation like

France has many vineyards.

France's Mediterranean coastline

oaks and grasses has been reduced to bare ground through ages of burning, woodcutting, and overgrazing. However, some plants still exist, such as the olive, oak, and pine trees. There is also an evergreen shrub called maquis that thrives in this area.

When France's woodlands were destroyed, many native animal species found themselves without homes. Many species of deer and fox, as well as wild boar, are still hunted and survive in multitude only in the deepest forest areas. The chamois, a type of goat, is found in the mountainous areas. There are also smaller animals like the porcupine, skunk, and marten, as well as many endangered species like beavers, otters, and lynx that still make their home in France.

Not only mammals but other animals as well make this country their home. Birds like ducks and geese spend the winters here before migrating to cooler climates for the summer. There are also many more exotic birds such as the flamingo and heron that live in the warmer Mediterranean region. While there are some reptiles, they are rare, and few are poisonous. The only poisonous reptile in France is the adder.

A stone rooster perches on a medieval church in central France.

2 FRANCE'S HISTORY AND GOVERNMENT

France has not always been the strong political power it is today. Throughout the ages, the land has been controlled by various groups and been the site of many bloody battles over its territories. Since prehistoric times, peoples have wanted to live in this fertile land.

PREHISTORIC FRANCE

The first inhabitants of France, at around 15,000 BCE, were **hunter-gatherers** traveling from place to place in search of food. These Stone Age tribes left behind evidence of their existence in the form of cave paintings. These drawings, found throughout the Pyrenees but most notably in the Lascaux caves, show the surprising technological advancement of the people of that time. Contrary to the stereotypes of cavemen as lumbering, unco-ordinated, almost monkey-like creatures, the amazing drawings on the cave walls show that the inhabitants of the area had fine motor skills and used forethought and creativity in planning their art. They also used tools like fine brushes and

Roman ruins are scattered across France.

paints to make these detailed drawings of animals and people.

By 6000 BCE, groups of settlers began to replace the migratory cultures in what is now France. These new peoples built a culture based on agriculture and farming, starting the process that would eventually change the country's landscape forever. Because this way of life was easier than how people had lived previously and could support more life, the population started to grow, increasing from four to five million by 1000 BCE. It was also around this time that metalworking was introduced, leading to the use of metals in such things as cooking pots and other tools.

Around 700 BCE, tribes from the north started invading the land. The largest group was the **Celts**, who spread throughout France, intermarrying and assimilating into the cultures that were already living there. Remnants of Celtic culture are still evident. For example, Gaul, a former name of what is now France, is derived from a Celtic word meaning "hero."

THE ROMAN EMPIRE

In the last century BCE, the Roman Empire attacked what is now France. The Romans organized their new holdings much as they did the rest of the empire, setting in place a judicial system as well as administration. Cities sprang up as a transportation system was established and the economy expanded. These cities were based on Rome itself and contained such buildings as temples, public baths, and marketplaces, some of which still survive.

As the cities spread their Roman culture to the more rural areas, Latin gradually replaced Gaulish as the country's language. Religious practices changed as well, with Roman cults replacing the **Druids** and Celtic religions. In 100 CE, Christianity began to spread throughout France, at first only in the cities, which were each under the control of a bishop, but later taking root throughout the country. However, government officials discouraged and even repressed the practice of Christianity.

DATING SYSTEMS AND THEIR MEANING

You might be accustomed to seeing dates expressed with the abbreviations BC or AD, as in the year 1000 BC or the year AD 1900. For centuries, this dating system has been the most common in the Western world. However, since BC and AD are based on Christianity (BC stands for Before Christ and AD stands for *anno Domini*, Latin for "in the year of our Lord"), many people now prefer to use abbreviations that people from all religions can be comfortable using. The abbreviations BCE (meaning Before Common Era) and CE (meaning Common Era) mark time in the same way (for example, 1000 BC is the same year as 1000 BCE, and AD 1900 is the same year as 1900 CE), but BCE and CE do not have the same religious overtones as BC and AD.

The Fall of the Roman Empire

Germanic tribes like the Franks and the Alemanni began to take over areas of Roman Gaul in the third century. At first, this seemed like a good thing for the failing empire, as the flow of immigrants to the country provided a new workforce. However, not all of these groups were content to enter the land peacefully, and the Romans were forced to **ally** with tribes like the Franks, Burgundians, and Visigoths in the fifth century. While this prevented the immediate collapse of the empire, it weakened it, and gradually the Romans lost power.

Although Gaul was now under Germanic control, its Roman occupation would have a lasting impact on the country. It was the first time the country was united under one government. The Romans had founded many cities, including Paris. Modern-day highways are built on old Roman roads, leading to some confusion, as some roads seem to meander aimlessly through cities and the countryside. Even the French language is based on Latin, although there are some Germanic and other influences apparent.

The Middle Ages

The immigration of these Germanic tribes into France marked the beginning of a period known as the Middle Ages. During the early period of this era, from about 350 to 1050, the state of the country declined; **literacy**, trade, and the legal system all deteriorated. However, not all aspects of life suffered. Many minorities achieved more rights during this era. Women were given the ability to maintain more control of property, and Jews, who had been persecuted under the Romans, were treated better under the Germanic kings.

Eventually, the Franks conquered the region that had once been Gaul and again gave the region a more centralized government. Led by Clovis, this group conquered much of present-day Germany and southeastern France. Clovis, realizing the importance of religion, converted to orthodox Christianity. At a time when most kings practiced Arianism, a type of Christianity not recognized by the Catholic Church, this made Clovis more agreeable to the pope, as well as making him more popular among his Christian subjects. His **precedent** led to centuries of rulers using Catholicism to aid them in their goals as leaders.

The Reformation

In 1517, Martin Luther began an attempt to reform the Catholic Church. This German theologian started a new belief system, Protestantism. In France, this new religion took many forms, the most popular one based on the teachings of John Calvin, a French **humanist**. The growing Protestant communities came to be known as Huguenots.

The government had mixed feelings about this new religion. Francis I, the monarch at the time, at first protected people suspected of being Protestants. As time went on, however, he eventually became more suspicious and less accepting. In the 1540s, thousands were tried and either put to death or sentenced to spend the rest of their lives rowing the galleys.

Christianity has played an important role in France's history.

At the same time, the Counter-Reformation traveled throughout France. This movement inspired reform of the existing Catholic Church, including the clergy and the development of new movements within the Church. Its goal was to again unite the nation under one faith—Catholicism.

In 1598, Henry IV issued the **Edict** of Nantes. This gave Protestants the right to practice their faith—under certain conditions. It also allowed them to have control of a few cities. However, this bill was so controversial that it was not registered for months. In the end, the edict did nothing to bring peace between the Protestants and Catholics. All it did was maintain the struggle at a less violent level.

The Enlightenment

The 1700s brought an increase in France's literacy rate. This helped bring about the Enlightenment, a period of growth that brought new ideas and concepts to the country. This movement was led by the *philosophes*, a group of scientists and thinkers who worked toward reform. They wrote pamphlets and books, the best known of which is the *Encyclopédie*, an international best seller.

Although these people worked together, they all had very different ideas about politics, agreeing only on the fact that liberty and freedom were desirable. Some, like Charles Louis de Montesquieu, believed this was most easily brought about through protecting the rights of the people as individuals. Voltaire represented another group, those who thought a strong monarchy could be used to bring about freedom. Some of the more radical, like philosopher Jean Jacques Rousseau, believed a democracy should be established and the monarchy abolished altogether. These new thinkers were part of what led to the French Revolution.

The French Revolution

Many factors caused the French Revolution. Among them was the fact that the king did not inspire much respect. Louis XV took little interest in the state of the country, leaving all the administrative decisions to his advisers. Instead, he seemed content to devote his attention to his many mistresses, especially the Marquise de Pompadour, who he refused to give up even when urged to by the court. Even after his death, the monarchy remained weak, with his son Louis XVI's only triumph being the American Revolution. Add this to the ideas spread by the Enlightenment and the hope for freedom inspired by the successful American Revolution, and the stage was set for change.

In 1788, the Estates-General decided to vote to give an equal vote to each estate, instead of basing it on the number of people in each estate. The Third Estate, which was formed from commoners and had the greatest number of representatives, saw this as an attempt to take power from them and give more to the First Estate (the nobles) and the Second Estate (the clergy). After arguing

A medieval watchtower in southern France

over this issue for weeks, the Third Estate struck out on its own, forming a new parliament it called the National Assembly in June. The other two estates were invited to join, as long as they agreed to vote by head instead of estate, and a crisis was averted. However, this break from tradition made the king look bad as he searched for a way to gain control over the situation.

Tensions deepened as a famine took hold in France. Peasants couldn't afford food as prices, especially that of bread, kept rising and rising. Finally, desperate Parisians attacked the Bastille on July 14, 1789, a day now celebrated as a national holiday in France. The Bastille, an old

The French nobility lived in manor houses like this one.

prison, served as a symbol of the monarchy and everything the people wanted to put down. The French Revolution had begun.

The French Revolution caused more problems than had been anticipated. The government changed completely, and revolution became almost acceptable in the political arena. Because of this, a peaceful end was harder to reach than had been expected.

In 1789, France started its journey to recovery. To this end, the Declaration of the Rights of Man and of the Citizen was written. This was the begin-

EUROPEAN UNION—FRANCE

ning of a constitution, finished in 1791, that enforced a limited monarchy and put most authority in the hands of a **unicameral** legislature.

During this time, a mob of upset citizens forced the royal family to leave the palace at Versailles and remain in Paris, where the king was made to accept the reforms of the people. In 1791, the king and his family tried to escape, but were stopped at the border of France, where they were returned to Paris virtually prisoners.

A new legislative body, the National Convention, voted to end the monarchy in 1792. In its place was to be a republic. The king was tried and put to death in January 1793.

Not all was peaceful among the members of the National Convention. In 1793, Maximillian Robespierre and his following of radical **Jacobeans** took over the parliament and started the Reign of Terror, a time meant to force citizens to help the republic. Over a quarter of a million people were arrested, and more than 30,000 guillotined, often for the most trivial of reasons or because they were alleged to have worked against the republic. Eventually, they had alienated the remainder of France so much that Robespierre and his advisers were executed, ending the Reign of Terror.

For the first time since the Revolution, a more moderate government was put in place. A new convention worked to keep the accomplishments of the Revolution, while keeping an event like the Terror from ever happening again. To this extent, a **bicameral** legislature was developed as well as an executive branch consisting of five members known as the Directory. Although this system worked for a while, it was ultimately unsuccessful, setting the stage for the next period in France's history: the rule of Napoleon Bonaparte.

NAPOLEON BONAPARTE

In 1799, Napoleon and his troops attacked the government, putting in place one of their own devising, called the Consulate. It consisted of Bonaparte and two others, but Napoleon was the one really in charge. After reforming the government, he declared himself emperor, and the country was back to where it had been before the Revolution.

At its height, Napoleon's First Empire went from Poland to Spain, as well as being allied with Russia, Prussia, and Austria. However, it didn't last long as countries used to independence rebelled. Perhaps one of Napoleon's biggest mistakes and one that led to his downfall was his attack of Russia in 1812, a mistake later repeated by Adolf Hitler during World War II. Caught in the middle of a Russian winter, Napoleon's troops quickly ran out of food and supplies; wagons were unable to get to them. The French troops never came into armed conflict with the Russians—the native troops retreated, burning any towns and cities that might have proved useful to the French. After thousands of his soldiers died from starvation and exposure, Napoleon was forced to admit defeat without reaching his destination of Moscow. By 1814, Napoleon was forced to abdicate his throne when armies invaded France. He was exiled to the island of Elba.

The year after, Napoleon tried to return. He came back to France, and for a short time, known as the Hundred Days, Napoleon gathered the people to him with talk of a more left-wing regime. However, at the Battle of Waterloo, Napoleon was defeated again. This time he was exiled to the island of Saint Helena, where he died in 1821.

THE INDUSTRIAL REVOLUTION

Unlike Great Britain, where the change from household industries to factories seemed to occur almost overnight, France's Industrial Revolution was more gradual. For many years, France was behind countries like Germany and Britain. Not only had France just gotten out of decades of revolutions, but it did not have as big a population growth as did other countries. One of the reasons for a lag in population growth was that the peasant class, almost extinct in other European countries, was still around. Because they were poor, family size was limited, leading to a lower birthrate. Therefore, there was less demand for more goods, because there were less people to ask for them, leaving no need for better, faster ways of production.

The Industrial Revolution started in the textile industry, as it did in many other countries. However, in the 1840s, the railway industry brought a boom throughout the economy. This also increased a demand for mining and metal ores to make rails. The Revolution eventually led to the development of a middle class, who worked mainly in small shops and professional jobs.

WORLD WAR I

France's involvement in World War I began in 1914, when German troops came through Belgium, looking to take control of Paris and defeat the French troops trying to retake Alsace-Lorraine from Germany. France's success in keeping the Germans from accomplishing their goals may have been the factor that kept the other side from winning quickly. Instead, a stalemate resulted that lasted for years, with neither side gaining much territory. The only result was the loss of thousands of lives.

The Treaty of Versailles, which ended the war, dictated the terms of peace. France regained control of Alsace-Lorraine, and Germany was forced to pay **reparations** for the war. Germany also had to agree to demilitarize the area between France and Germany known as the Rhineland, which France could occupy until 1935.

World War I led to another decline in France's birthrate as millions of men returned home wounded or, worse, didn't return home at all. Immigrants came into the country to take the jobs left behind by the lost soldiers. During the war, women had been allowed to work in factories, but were now pushed out of their jobs to make room for veterans. There were also economic losses as the area that Germany had taken over contained more than half of the steel and coal industries. Coupled with the economic cost of the war itself, debt increased and the value of the franc weakened.

In 1928, France joined the League of Nations in an attempt to stave off another war. However, this organization was weak and had no real power, partly because the United States refused to join.

French veterans remember the role the nation played in the world wars.

WORLD WAR II

In 1939, after numerous violations by Germany of the Treaty of Versailles, and despite the League of Nations' attempts at **appeasement**, war was declared on that country. At first, France maintained its neutrality. Then, in 1940, Hitler attacked France. Unlike what had happened in World War I, this was a decisive victory for Germany, and France became an occupied country.

In 1918, France signed an **armistice** saying that they would demobilize their armed forces, basically giving over the northern two-thirds of the country to Germany. Despite ceding to all of Germany's demands, the country still suffered. Thousands of forced laborers worked in Germany, and the country was forced to give money to help support the German war effort. In 1942, Germany took control over the remainder of France, resulting in a French puppet government.

Vichy, the government at the time, was almost as bad as the Germans. While not actively involved in **genocide**, anti-Semitism was rampant, and Jews were forced to give up their jobs and property. Some Jews were sent to Germany, where they were placed in death camps.

Although most people supported the French government at first, people began resisting German control. Charles de Gaulle, the former undersecretary of war, escaped to Paris, where he formed a government in exile. Groups of people fought against the Germans, sabotaging the war effort and secretly communicating with de Gaulle.

France was liberated in 1944 after Allied troops landed at Normandy. A new provisional government, led by de Gaulle, assumed power.

FRANCE AND THE EUROPEAN UNION

France was a founding member of the European Union (EU), which was established by the Maastricht Treaty in 1991, which went into effect in 1993 after the treaty was ratified by all member nations. The country had its six-month term as president during the last half of 2000.

As well as helping to put in place the EU, now one of the most influential organizations in the world, France also founded many of the preceding organizations and treaties, such as the European Coal and Steel Community (ECSC) and the European Community (EC).

FRANCE'S GOVERNMENT TODAY

France's modern government consists of a republic led by a president, much like the United States. The current form of government was established with a new constitution in 1958, one that gave more power to the president and less to parliament.

The president is elected by popular vote; there is no **electoral college** as in the United States. The president is the head of state and of the country, but he must appoint a prime minister who takes over the task of controlling the government. The legislative branch of the government is bicameral;

parliament is made up of the National Assembly and the Senate, which has slightly less influence. There is also the Constitutional Council, a judicial branch of the government that supervises elections and decides the constitutionality of laws.

Amendments to the constitution may come about in many different ways. The president can propose an amendment, or the government or members of parliament may request one. However the amendment is proposed, it must have the approval of both branches of the parliament and be approved in a referendum.

There are three levels of local government: communes, departments, and regions. Communes are the smallest and can range in size from one small village to a piece of a larger city. Then there are departments, most of them named after the geographical area where they are. These departments make up the regions, the largest piece of the local governments. No matter what the size, all of these have their own elected legislative and executive branches.

A medieval castle off the coast of Antibes reminds modern French citizens of their past.

Vacationers from around the world flock to Nice's warm beaches and fancy restaurants.

3 THE ECONOMY

While French industry consisted of mainly farms and small businesses until the 1940s, after World War II, the government set in place a plan designed to modernize the economy. These reforms consisted of nationalizing different industries, including energy production, the banking system, and many factories and other manufacturing fields. This, along with France's induction into the EC—the forerunner of the EU—led to a period of economic growth in the past twenty-five years. Today, France boasts the world's fifth-strongest economy, behind only the United States, Japan, Germany, and the United Kingdom.

As of 2003, France's **gross domestic product (GDP)** was equivalent to 1.737 trillion American dollars. Per capita income is US$28,700. Though this may seem like a lot of money, not everyone earns this much. This is an average figure—the average amount an average French citizen earns in a year; many people earn far below this amount, while others earn much more.

ENTRANCE INTO THE EU

The creation of the EU put in place a single market in Europe for producers to sell their goods and

France's medieval castles attract visitors from around the world, making tourism an important factor in the nation's economy.

services. Though this has allowed people, capital, and goods to move freely throughout Europe, there have been some downfalls. French businesses, used to protection by trade barriers, have become more competitive in order to survive in the wider marketplace.

The formation of the EU also brought about the adoption of the euro. This common currency makes it even easier for people and goods to travel from one country to another.

SOCIALISM: HOW MUCH CONTROL SHOULD THE GOVERNMENT HAVE?

Various French governments have tried different variations of government control of the economy. In 1982, François Mitterrand, then the president of the country, attempted to **nationalize** most of the economy. At the height of this socialist plan, the state owned thirteen of twenty of the major corporations in France.

Since then, the government has begun to encourage limited privatization of businesses. Now France tends toward a mixed economy, a system in which both government and private sectors share control of various industries.

Although there is some private ownership of goods and services in the economy, the government is still involved, using its influence to make sure the economy is growing and stable. France used fiscal policies, such as cutting taxes and increasing government spending, to increase demand for goods by giving people more money to spend and therefore encouraging the economy to grow. However, this policy often results in a budget deficit, with the government spending more than it takes in, and in 2003, France received a warning from the EU to restrain its government spending and keep under the 3 percent budget deficit limit the EU has set in place.

TAXES AND OTHER INCOMES

The French government gets income from many sources, including taxes. Things like sales tax and income tax provide the government with money. There is also a wealth tax in France, which those with assets worth more than 732,000 euro must pay. All in all, France is one of the most heavily taxed nations in the EU.

A large part of the GDP comes from government expenditure. Social security, the wages of government employees, debt service on the national debt, and investment all contribute to the money people make from the federal government.

THE LABOR FORCE

The structure of the economy has changed drastically in recent years. In the 1950s, most French workers had jobs in agriculture or industry. Now, however, the **service sector** is the most popular, employing 74.1 percent of France's labor force of 27 million people. The highest numbers of new jobs are in the education, health, and public administration fields.

ECONOMIC SECTORS

France is the EU's leading producer of agricultural goods, with more than 48.4 million acres (19.6 million hectares) used for farming. The country produces dairy products, beef, wheat, oilseeds, fruits and vegetables, and wine.

The reason France is able to produce so many different products is because the country is so well suited to agriculture. There is fertile soil, plentiful rain, and a long growing season. The variety comes from regional differences in climate—in the northwest, where it is cooler and wetter, there are grasslands for cattle to graze on, while in the Mediterranean region, where it is warm and dry, it is easy to grow various types of grapes.

The Common Agricultural Policy (CAP) was put in place in 1957 with the creation of the European Economic Community (EEC). This created a system of common prices across what is now the EU, leading to greater agricultural production and helping many farmers improve their incomes. Because France is the leading agricultural country in the EU, it benefits the most from these funds.

France also is a mining country, the second-largest producer of iron ore in Western Europe. This was once a major source of employment, but production decreased when it was discovered that French iron has many impurities. However, other metals and minerals—such as uranium, aluminum, salt, gypsum, tungsten, and sulfur—are still mined. Coal is also mined, although on a much smaller scale than during the turn of the twentieth century. There are also stone quarries that provide such materials as sand, gravel, stone, and clay.

Manufacturing is another major industry in France. It accounts for the main source of income through exports and produces such goods as food products, automobiles, airplanes, ships, trains, machinery, chemicals, and textiles. The country is well known for its innovations in the transportation sectors; the French TGV (*Train á Grande Vitesse* or Train of Great Speed) is one of the world's fastest passenger trains.

People from all over the world come to France to visit, making tourism an important part of the service sector. In 2003, France was the most visited nation in the world, with more than 75 million people coming to see this beautiful and historic nation. The French themselves travel around their own country, taking advantage of the five-week paid vacation all French workers must receive, to experience a different part of France.

TRANSPORTATION

France enjoys a well-maintained network of highways, railroads, and waterways. The country's dense system of roads make it home to one of the best transportation systems in the world. It was the first country in the EU to have fast railroads available for passengers. The Metro systems in the cities, most notably Paris, are easy to use and very comfortable.

Paris is the center of the transportation system. It is home to a major airport—Charles de Gaulle—and all of France's major roads and waterways lead from the city. Recently, however, efforts have been made to connect other larger cities while skipping Paris.

France's fertile farmland

France has more than 5,300 miles (8,500 kilometers) of navigable rivers and canals, making it the longest system of water transportation in Europe. Because most of these canals were built in the 1800s and today's large ships cannot fit, water transport of goods has decreased in the last decades as other alternatives, such as air transportation, have become cheaper and easier. There are many seaports in France, such as those at Marseille and Le Havre, which are the entry points for the country's imports of petroleum.

ENERGY

France has few natural energy resources of its own, relying mainly on imported petroleum.

ing on foreign oil, and the government started developing alternative energy sources.

France found that it could use nuclear power to make its own energy, thereby reducing the amount it needed to import from other countries. As of 2002, France's nuclear power plants produced 78.5 percent of its power; after the United States, France is the largest producer of nuclear power plants. While this has met with few protests, not all attempts to harness this type of power have been successful. In southeastern France, a plant was closed in 1998 after technical problems and safety concerns, along with protests from various environmental groups.

Not all of France's electricity comes from nuclear power; the country also uses hydroelectric and thermal power. France produces more energy than it needs, exporting the excess to the countries around it, such as the UK, Italy, and Switzerland.

QUICK FACTS: THE ECONOMY OF FRANCE

Gross Domestic Product (GDP): US$1.737 trillion
GDP per capita: US$28,700
Industries: machinery, chemicals, automobiles, metallurgy, aircraft, electronics; textiles, food processing; tourism
Agriculture: wheat, cereals, sugar beets, potatoes, wine grapes; beef, dairy products; fish
Export commodities: machinery and transportation equipment, aircraft, plastics, chemicals, pharmaceutical products, iron and steel, beverages
Export partners: Germany 15%, Spain 9.4%, UK 9.3%, Italy 9%, Belgium 7.2%, U.S. 6.7%
Import commodities: machinery and equipment, vehicles, crude oil, aircraft, plastics, chemicals
Import partners: Germany 19.2%, Belgium 9.8%, Italy 8.8%, Spain 7.3%, UK 7%, Netherlands 6.7%, U.S. 5.1%
Currency: euro
Currency exchange rate: US$1 = .82 euro (August 1, 2005)

Note: All figures are from 2004 unless otherwise noted.
Source: www.cia.gov, 2005.

While the country was able to mine coal during the Industrial Revolution, this power source was quickly outdated as gasoline developed, and gasoline is a scarce commodity in France. In 1973, the oil crisis showed the pitfalls of depend-

ECONOMIC PROBLEMS

While France has a strong economy, the country still has many problems. One of these is the high unemployment rate. From the mid-1970s, the number of people without jobs has been consistently over 10 percent, falling slightly to 9 percent in 2002. While some unemployment is necessary, and even helpful to the economy, the rate of full employment is usu-

France has well-maintained highways.

ally considered around 5 percent—half that of France. France has taken many measures to lower unemployment, but with limited success; among these efforts was a law that reduced the workweek from thirty-nine to thirty-five hours (which means that more workers would be needed to accomplish the same tasks, creating more jobs).

Because the economy is not growing very fast, it is getting harder and harder for France to maintain its welfare system, which has traditionally been extremely generous to its citizens. France is finding it necessary to reform this system, delicately balancing the benefits each person may receive with a solution that is agreeable to the public.

France has come a long way since its economy consisted mostly of family farms. However, some things don't change; France is still a farming country, producing the most agricultural goods in Western Europe.

A young French boy fishing in Antibes

4 FRANCE'S PEOPLE AND CULTURE

CHAPTER

France is home to 60,656,178 people, making it the fourth-most populated nation in Europe. While many people live here, it is also the largest nation in Western Europe, meaning that the population density is still less than in most European nations, with 288 people per square mile (111 people per square kilometer).

ETHNICITIES

Although most people in the country are French, they have varied ethnic backgrounds. Hundreds of years of invading groups have left their mark, including the Romans, Celts, and Franks, from whom the name France comes.

The French government has tried hard to **assimilate** minorities and has come a long way from the French Revolution when less than half of the people spoke French. After the Revolution, in an attempt to find unity, the government declared that if a person lived in France, they were French. This was part of the government's effort to make a nation based on a common language. This worked until the formation of the EU, which forced France for the first time to acknowledge and offer rights to minorities.

Many ethnic minorities are descended from ancient peoples and live on the same land their ancestors have inhabited for centuries. For example, in the northern part of France live a group called the Flemings, who live around the town of Dunkerque. They speak mainly a **dialect** of Dutch and have assimilated without protest into French culture. On the other hand, the Bretons, who have Celtic blood and live in Brittany, seek to have their own culture and way of life. To this extent they differentiate themselves from the French by incorporating their Celtic heritage into their lives and setting up schools in their own language.

Immigrants from all over the world make up approximately 7.5 percent of France's population. The largest immigrant group is from North Africa, including the Islamic nations of Algeria, Morocco, and Tunisia. There are more than 4 million Muslims in France, many from Africa or Turkey and who live in France's cities. This has led to much debate as people argue over whether or not traditional Islamic head coverings should be allowed in school. In 2004, a law was passed forbidding schoolchildren from wearing religious symbols; many Muslims felt the law was targeting them.

LANGUAGE

French is the official language of France. The language is a dialect of the ancient *langue d'oïl*, which originated in what is now northern France. Other, regional languages are spoken as well, the most widespread of which is Occitan, the *langue d'oc* (Languedoc), which is spoken mainly in southern France. Almost 6 million speak *Provençal*, the major dialect. However, most people speak mainstream French as well.

Other languages include German in the region of Alsace; Breton in Brittany; Catalan, and Basque, which are based in the Pyrenees; Flemish, which is based on Dutch; and Corse, an Italian dialect spoken on the island of Corsica. Many of France's immigrants also speak their native languages, most notably Arabic and Turkish.

RELIGION IN FRANCE

The most popular religion in France is Roman Catholicism, with more than 80 percent of the population claiming to practice this faith. However, while many identify with this religion and its culture, only a few—about 5 percent—actively practice it.

Islam is France's second-largest faith, with about 5 percent of the population Muslim. There are also some Protestants, although these are a minority. Protestants fled France in the sixteenth and seventeenth centuries because of persecution from the Catholics; not many returned. There is also a small Jewish minority. However, more than 10 percent of the French people claim to have no religion at all.

The government supported both Christianity and Judaism until the beginning of the twentieth century. In 1905, church and state were officially separated. Because many people opposed the

Christianity is important to France's history and culture.

Catholic Church and their control over schools and the educational system, the government was forbidden to pay public funds to any religious official or clergy. Therefore, the state cannot officially recognize any religion.

EDUCATION

Basic schooling is guaranteed for all French citizens. Students must attend school from ages six to sixteen, and all schools are free. Universities are also free to those students who qualify. There is also an extensive system of private schools, many controlled by the Catholic Church. One out of six children attend these schools.

Education starts out with two or three years of preschool, which is optional. Students go on to a primary, or elementary school until they are eleven. After the *collège*, or middle school, which students attend until they are fifteen, they go on to *lyceé*, or high school. Here teens have a choice. There are general schools, which are much like those in the United States, offering a well-rounded education in all the subjects. Students attend these general schools for three years, ending with a nationwide exam. If students pass this exam, they earn the *baccalauréate* degree needed to enter a university. This is a hard exam; only two-thirds of those who take it pass, and the others must take it over again. Students can also decide to go to a technical or vocational school and earn a professional certificate/diploma after one to three years.

The system of universities is expanding, adding new colleges apart from the general, traditional university. One such type is the technological institutes, or *instututs universitaires de technologie*. They specialize in such fields as engineering and other technology-related majors. Community colleges have also developed in smaller cities and towns.

Besides colleges and universities, there are graduate schools, called *grandes écoles*. These are extremely hard to get into; applicants must pass competitive exams.

SPORTS

The French people are very active, loving physical activity of all kinds. While professional sports like soccer (called *le foot*) and bicycle racing are extremely popular, many people belong to sports clubs where they play for fun. The most widespread of these clubs allow members to play soccer, tennis, basketball, or *boules*.

The Tour de France is the world's most famous bicycle race. Each year such legends as Lance Armstrong gather to compete for the prize. The French Open, one of tennis's Grand Slam events, attracts visitors from around the world to the clay courts of Roland-Garros Stadium in Paris.

France is famous for its wine and cheese.

FRENCH FOOD

It is a not uncommon to see French people sitting at sidewalk cafés, enjoying a cup of coffee or Orangina, a popular French drink, while they watch the passersby or read the paper. These small restaurants are all over France, pointing to the emphasis the culture places on food.

France is famous for its food; the country has many regional dishes that can be found nowhere else in the world. Some of the more popular foods that have become internationally known include quiches; crêpes; bouillabaisse, a fish soup; and pâté de foie gras, a spread made of goose livers. French bread is also known for its taste; most people go every day to *boulangeries* to get fresh baked goods.

Unlike Americans, whose largest meal of the day tends to be eaten in the evening, the French eat a small breakfast, a big lunch, and a small dinner. For special occasions, however, huge, multi-course meals are served, lasting from around 8 P.M. until sometimes very early in the morning. These elaborate dinners consist of appetizers, one or two main courses, a salad, fruits and cheeses, and then dessert. Of course, various types of wine are served throughout the meal.

An example of French medieval architecture

FESTIVALS AND HOLIDAYS

Because much of French culture is based on Roman Catholicism, many of the holidays celebrated have a religious base. Christmas and Easter are celebrated much as they are in the United States. However, a festival with a uniquely French flavor is Mardi Gras, or Fat Tuesday. This is the day before Lent (the forty days preceding Easter) begins and marks the end of the Carnival season. Parades, music, costumes, and food highlight the festivities, as people rush to celebrate before the traditional season of fasting and prayer.

The national holiday in France is Bastille Day on July 14. This celebrates the fall of the Bastille and the success of the common people in the French Revolution. There are many regional festivals, celebrating everything from food to film and from music to another successful harvest.

THE ARTS: ARCHITECTURE, PAINTING, MUSIC, AND LITERATURE

France has produced many famous artists, as well as developing whole movements of painting. One such style is Impressionism, a movement of the late nineteenth and early twentieth centuries. The movement got its name from Claude Monet's painting *Impressionist Sunrise*. Although he refused to call himself an Impressionist, one of the first practitioners of the technique was Édouard Manet. Pierre Auguste Renoir is one of Impressionism's most famous artists.

QUICK FACTS: THE PEOPLE OF FRANCE

Population: 60,656,178
Ethnic groups: Celtic and Latin with Teutonic, Slavic, North African, Indochinese, Basque minorities
Age structure:
    0–14 years: 18.4%
    15–64 years: 65.2%
    65 years and over: 16.4%
Population growth rate: 0.37%
Birth rate: 12.15 births/1,000 pop.
Death rate: 9.08 deaths/1,000 pop.
Migration rate: 0.66 migrant(s)/1,000 pop.
Infant mortality rate: 4.26 deaths/1,000 live births
Life expectancy at birth:
    Total population: 79.6 years
    Male: 75.96 years
    Female: 83.42 years
Total fertility rate: 1.85 children born/woman
Religions: Roman Catholic 83–88%, Protestant 2%, Jewish 1%, Muslim 5–10%, unaffiliated 4%
Languages: French
Literacy rate: 99% (1980)

Note: All figures are from 2005 unless otherwise noted.
Source: www.cia.gov, 2005.

Medieval French painters portrayed fanciful creatures on a church ceiling in Fréjus.

However, French painters have won prestige throughout history, from Baroque artists like Georges de la Tour and Claude Lorrain to Romantic painters like Eugène Delacroix. In the twentieth century, Henri Matisse, Pierre Bonnard, and Marcel Duchamp became famous for their modern works.

Painting is not the only art form at which the French excel. The country is rife with examples of great architecture, the earliest examples being its Gothic churches, built between the twelfth and fifteenth centuries. The palace of Versailles is a great example of the luxury of the neoclassical era, and, of course, the Eiffel Tower shows the talent of the nineteenth-century Charles Garnier.

Since the eleventh century, French musicians have been singing of noble deeds and quests in the form of *chansons de geste*. Throughout history France has continued this musical tradition, creating new forms of music and raising famous composers. In the 1300s, composer Guillaume de Machaut developed the polyphonic form of music, or the idea that music could have more than one part. Famous French musicians and composers include Georges Bizet, Camille Saint-Saëns, Gabriel Fauré, and Claude Debussy. The French continue to enjoy music, and newer forms are popular today, including rock and pop hits.

French literature has been world famous for centuries. Writers such as Marcel Proust and Albert Camus continue to be popular. The country is also home to many books for a younger audience; children all over the world read *The Little Prince* by Antoine de Saint Exupéry.

Antibes, a resort town west of Nice

5 CHAPTER THE CITIES

Although many of France's people live on farms and in small towns, the cities are part of what makes France so unique. Millions of people live in the capital of Paris, as well as other cities scattered throughout the country.

PARIS

As well as being France's capital, Paris is also the country's largest city. Home to more than 2 million people, Paris is an important cultural, economic, and political center. The city is the seat of the national government and contains many famous landmarks and museums inside its borders.

The Eiffel Tower is the most visible landmark in Paris, towering 984 feet (300 meters) over the rest of the city. Built in 1889, this monument was built for the Universal Exhibition in celebration of the French Revolution. Between 1889 and 2002, more than 200 million people visited the Eiffel Tower.

Paris is also home to the Louvre, the famous art museum perhaps best known for its display of the *Mona Lisa*. However, this is not all the museum has to offer. The Louvre has exhibits displaying the art from Neolithic times to the present.

Fast Facts

The Eiffel Tower weighs more than 10,000 tons; took 2 years, 2 months, and 5 days to construct; and has 1,665 steps.

Like most international centers of commerce and government, this city can be a little overwhelming at first. Cars rush by, seemingly bent on getting to where they need to go as fast as possible, all the while ignoring such trivialities as traffic lanes or stop signs. Then, once they reach their destination, it is not uncommon to see vehicles parked wherever there is room, even on the sidewalk.

Among all the bustle and glamour of the city, it is sometimes hard to remember the history that is Paris. The catacombs under the city provide a glimpse into what Paris used to be like. These huge caverns extend throughout the city, and some have lasted for more than 2,000 years. However, not all of this underground system is visible to the public. One can go see, however, mass graves from the eighteenth century. It was at this time that the government of Paris realized their cemeteries were desperately overcrowded, and the transportation of bodies to graveyards leftover from medieval times was providing a threat to the health of the people of Paris. So, they converted some of the old, underground tunnels into mass gravesites, even going so far as to carry millions of already buried bodies from the cemetery that was already in place to the new site.

Paris is a multifaceted city. On the surface is the rush of a city famous for its fashion and commerce. People hurry from place to place, never stopping to look up. On the other hand, Paris is a tourist attraction, full of various monuments and museums and impossible to fully enjoy no matter how long you spend there. And the action doesn't stop when darkness falls; Paris's nickname, the City of Lights, is well earned. Paris has something for everyone who visits, and no one will ever forget a visit there.

MARSEILLE

Marseille, on the Mediterranean coast, is the second-largest city in France. Founded in the sixth century BCE by Greek sailors, the city continues to be a home to diverse groups of ethnicities.

Marseille leads the health sector in France, home to a hospital complex that provides research

Paris is famous for its Eiffel Tower.

and develops new equipment benefiting people all over the world. While it is a high-tech city, providing cutting-edge research, it is also a place that has been populated for more than 2,600 years, and as such is full of traditions and festivals.

The city is famous for its soap, as well as its production of *santons*—clay characters based on well-known figures of the area—that are put in Christmas crèches. The people of Marseille love to party and have numerous celebrations throughout the year, including a Candlemas festival where boat-shaped cookies called *navettes* are eaten, a kite-flying festival, and a Garlic Fair.

Because of its location on the Mediterranean Sea, Marseille is a popular tourist destination. People come from all over the world not only to enjoy the mild climate and take advantage of the many water sports available in the area, but also to catch a glimpse of some of the breathtaking views around the city. Marseille also serves as a gateway; the rest of Provence is easy to travel to, making it an easy place around which to center one's trip.

LYON

Lyon is an important manufacturing center, historically famous for its textiles and fabric production. Now, however, other industries have become more predominant, including chemical production, automobiles, and gasoline. Found where two

Montpellier, France's 8th largest city, is a center for medical and university study.

major rivers, the Saône and the Rhône, meet, Lyon is the third-largest city in France and boasts a population of just under 500,000. Because the city is located conveniently at the joint of two major rivers, it has been a center of trade since its origins as a safe haven for the Celts.

While it is true that the textile industry, most notably the production of silk, has declined slightly in recent years, it still provides an important part of the culture of Lyon. Many well-known designers have their base in the city, which sports many museums about the history of this art and provides courses in design to anyone who is interested.

The home of Christianity in what was formerly Gaul, Lyon provided an important stepping-stone in the spread of this religion. Today, this is evident in the many ancient cathedrals that stand throughout the city. However, though Christianity is an important part of Lyon's heritage, the city prides itself on its religious tolerance; the city is home to many different religions, all able to coexist peacefully.

On December eighth, the Feast of Immaculate Conception, the city of Lyon lights up, with different-colored lights on more than 200 of its important monuments, bridges, and buildings. This celebration stems from 1852, when the old bell tower on the ancient Chapel of Fourvière was restored. Because of rain on the night it was to be blessed, the bishop decided to cancel the light show that had been planned. Instead, the people of Lyon, without any planning at all, lit candles and lamps in their windows to celebrate this momentous

occasion. Today, shopkeepers decorate the windows of their stores, and cruises allow visitors to see Lyon from the river.

Lyon is also a popular tourist destination, surrounded by beautiful mountains and near France's famous wine region. With its unique flavor and reputation in the fashion industry, it is no wonder that this city attracts people from all over.

NICE

Nice is mainly a resort city as evidenced by its expensive hotels, restaurants of all kinds, and, of course, the casinos. While the new city is much like any other city, either in France or anywhere else in the world, the old city is totally different. It's like stepping into another world; all of a sudden antique buildings line the narrow streets—a much different feeling from the wide avenues, highways, and the more modern architecture in the rest of the city.

Perhaps Nice's most famous tradition is Carnival, a wild, ten-day celebration that signals the beginning of Lent. Begun in the Middle Ages, Carnival involves lots of parades, concerts, and food before people start fasting and setting their minds on the death of Jesus Christ. Each year, a king and a queen are crowned and are presented to their subjects in a parade with spectacular floats.

Like many other French cities, Nice contains traces of its past. Ancient Roman remains can still be seen in parts of the town, showing that the past is never truly gone.

The EU flag

6

The Formation of the European Union

The EU is an economic and political confederation of twenty-five European nations. Member countries abide by common foreign and security policies and cooperate on judicial and domestic affairs. The confederation, however, does not replace existing states or governments. Each of the twenty-five member states is **autonomous**, but they have all agreed to establish some common institutions and to hand over some of their own decision-making powers to these international bodies. As a result, decisions on matters that interest all member states can be made democratically, accommodating everyone's concerns and interests.

Today, the EU is the most powerful regional organization in the world. It has evolved from a primarily economic organization to an increasingly political one. Besides promoting economic cooperation, the EU requires that its members uphold fundamental values of peace and **solidarity**, human dignity, freedom, and equality. Based on the principles of democracy and the rule of law, the EU respects the culture and organizations of member states.

History

The seeds of the EU were planted more than fifty years ago in a Europe reduced to smoking piles of rubble by two world wars. European nations suffered great financial difficulties in the postwar period. They were struggling to get back on their feet and realized that another war would cause further hardship. Knowing that internal conflict was hurting all of Europe, a drive began toward European cooperation.

France took the first historic step. On May 9, 1950 (now celebrated as Europe Day), Robert Schuman, the French foreign minister, proposed the coal and steel industries of France and West Germany be coordinated under a single supranational authority. The proposal, known as the Treaty of Paris, attracted four other countries—Belgium, Luxembourg, the Netherlands, and Italy—and resulted in the 1951 formation of the European Coal and Steel Community (ECSC). These six countries became the founding members of the EU.

In 1957, European cooperation took its next big leap. Under the Treaty of Rome, the European Economic Community (EEC) and the European Atomic Energy Community (EURATOM) were formed. Informally known as the Common Market, the EEC promoted joining the national economies into a single European economy. The 1965 Treaty of Brussels (more commonly referred to as the Merger Treaty) united these various treaty organizations under a single umbrella, the European Community (EC).

In 1992, the Maastricht Treaty (also known as the Treaty of the European Union) was signed in Maastricht, the Netherlands, signaling the birth of the EU as it stands today. **Ratified** the following year, the Maastricht Treaty provided for a central banking system, a common currency (the euro) to replace the national currencies, a legal definition of the EU, and a framework for expanding the

The EU's united economy has allowed it to become a worldwide financial power.

EU's political role, particularly in the area of foreign and security policy.

By 1993, the member countries completed their move toward a single market and agreed to participate in a larger common market, the European Economic Area, established in 1994.

The EU, headquartered in Brussels, Belgium, reached its current member strength in spurts. In

CHAPTER SIX—THE FORMATION OF THE EUROPEAN UNION

© BCE ECB EZB EKT EKP 2002

© BCE ECB EZB EKT EKP 2002

© BCE ECB EZB EKT EKP 2002

© BCE ECB EZB EKT EKP 2002

The euro, the EU's currency

1973, Denmark, Ireland, and the United Kingdom joined the six founding members of the EC. They were followed by Greece in 1981, and Portugal and Spain in 1986. The 1990s saw the unification of the two Germanys, and as a result, East Germany entered the EU fold. Austria, Finland, and Sweden joined the EU in 1995, bringing the total number of member states to fifteen. In 2004, the EU nearly doubled its size when ten countries—Cyprus, the Czech Republic, Estonia, Hungary, Latvia, Lithuania, Malta, Poland, Slovakia, and Slovenia—became members.

THE EU FRAMEWORK

The EU's structure has often been compared to a "roof of a temple with three columns." As established by the Maastricht Treaty, this three-pillar framework encompasses all the policy areas—or pillars—of European cooperation. The three pillars of the EU are the European Community, the Common Foreign and Security Policy (CFSP), and Police and Judicial Co-operation in Criminal Matters.

QUICK FACTS: THE EUROPEAN UNION

Number of Member Countries: 25

Official Languages: 20—Czech, Danish, Dutch, English, Estonian, Finnish, French, German, Greek, Hungarian, Italian, Latvian, Lithuanian, Maltese, Polish, Portuguese, Slovak, Slovenian, Spanish, and Swedish; additional language for treaty purposes: Irish Gaelic

Motto: *In Varietate Concordia* (United in Diversity)

European Council's President: Each member state takes a turn to lead the council's activities for 6 months.

European Commission's President: José Manuel Barroso (Portugal)

European Parliament's President: Josep Borrell (Spain)

Total Area: 1,502,966 square miles (3,892,685 sq. km.)

Population: 454,900,000

Population Density: 302.7 people/square mile (116.8 people/sq. km.)

GDP: €9.61.1012

Per Capita GDP: €21,125

Formation:
- Declared: February 7, 1992, with signing of the Maastricht Treaty
- Recognized: November 1, 1993, with the ratification of the Maastricht Treaty

Community Currency: Euro. Currently 12 of the 25 member states have adopted the euro as their currency.

Anthem: "Ode to Joy"

Flag: Blue background with 12 gold stars arranged in a circle

Official Day: Europe Day, May 9

Source: europa.eu.int

Pillar One

The European Community pillar deals with economic, social, and environmental policies. It is a body consisting of the European Parliament, European Commission, European Court of Justice, Council of the European Union, and the European Courts of Auditors.

Pillar Two

The idea that the EU should speak with one voice in world affairs is as old as the European integration process itself. Toward this end, the Common Foreign and Security Policy (CFSP) was formed in 1993.

PILLAR THREE

The cooperation of EU member states in judicial and criminal matters ensures that its citizens enjoy the freedom to travel, work, and live securely and safely anywhere within the EU. The third pillar—Police and Judicial Co-operation in Criminal Matters—helps to protect EU citizens from international crime and to ensure equal access to justice and fundamental rights across the EU.

The flags of the EU's nations:

top row, left to right
Belgium, the Czech Republic, Denmark, Germany, Estonia, Greece

second row, left to right
Spain, France, Ireland, Italy, Cyprus, Latvia

third row, left to right
Lithuania, Luxembourg, Hungary, Malta, the Netherlands, Austria

bottom row, left to right
Poland, Portugal, Slovenia, Slovakia, Finland, Sweden, United Kingdom

ECONOMIC STATUS

As of May 2004, the EU had the largest economy in the world, followed closely by the United States. But even though the EU continues to enjoy a trade surplus, it faces the twin problems of high unemployment rates and **stagnancy**.

The 2004 addition of ten new member states is expected to boost economic growth. EU membership is likely to stimulate the economies of these relatively poor countries. In turn, their prosperity growth will be beneficial to the EU.

THE EURO

The EU's official currency is the euro, which came into circulation on January 1, 2002. The shift to the euro has been the largest monetary changeover in the world. Twelve countries—Belgium, Germany, Greece, Spain, France, Ireland, Italy, Luxembourg, the Netherlands, Finland, Portugal, and Austria—have adopted it as their currency.

SINGLE MARKET

Within the EU, laws of member states are harmonized and domestic policies are coordinated to create a larger, more-efficient single market.

The chief features of the EU's internal policy on the single market are:

- free trade of goods and services

- a common EU competition law that controls anticompetitive activities of companies and member states

- removal of internal border control and harmonization of external controls between member states

- freedom for citizens to live and work anywhere in the EU as long as they are not dependent on the state

- free movement of **capital** between member states

- harmonization of government regulations, corporation law, and trademark registration

- a single currency

- coordination of environmental policy

- a common agricultural policy and a common fisheries policy

- a common system of indirect taxation, the value-added tax (VAT), and common customs duties and **excise**

- funding for research

- funding for aid to disadvantaged regions

The EU's external policy on the single market specifies:

- a common external **tariff** and a common position in international trade negotiations

- funding of programs in other Eastern European countries and developing countries

COOPERATION AREAS

EU member states cooperate in other areas as well. Member states can vote in European Parliament elections. Intelligence sharing and cooperation in criminal matters are carried out through EUROPOL and the Schengen Information System.

The EU is working to develop common foreign and security policies. Many member states are resisting such a move, however, saying these are sensitive areas best left to individual member states. Arguing in favor of a common approach to security and foreign policy are countries like France and Germany, who insist that a safer and more secure Europe can only become a reality under the EU umbrella.

One of the EU's great achievements has been to create a boundary-free area within which people, goods, services, and money can move around freely; this ease of movement is sometimes called "the four freedoms." As the EU grows in size, so do the challenges facing it—and yet its fifty-year history has amply demonstrated the power of cooperation.

 EUROPEAN UNION—FRANCE

Europe is proud of its "bright idea," a union with economic and political power.

The EU believes that it can use its power to act as a "lighthouse" for the rest of the world.

KEY EU INSTITUTIONS

Five key institutions play a specific role in the EU.

THE EUROPEAN PARLIAMENT

The European Parliament (EP) is the democratic voice of the people of Europe. Directly elected every five years, the Members of the European Parliament (MEPs) sit not in national ***blocs*** but in political groups representing the seven main political parties of the member states. Each group reflects the political ideology of the national parties to which its members belong. Some MEPs are not attached to any political group.

COUNCIL OF THE EUROPEAN UNION

The Council of the European Union (formerly known as the Council of Ministers) is the main legislative and decision-making body in the EU. It brings together the nationally elected representatives of the member-state governments. One minister from each of the EU's member states attends council meetings. It is the forum in which government representatives can assert their interests and reach compromises. Increasingly, the Council of the European Union and the EP are acting together as colegislators in decision-making processes.

EUROPEAN COMMISSION

The European Commission does much of the day-to-day work of the EU. Politically independent, the commission represents the interests of the EU as a whole, rather than those of individual member states. It drafts proposals for new European laws, which it presents to the EP and the Council of the European Union. The European Commission makes sure EU decisions are implemented properly and supervises the way EU funds are spent. It also sees that everyone abides by the European treaties and European law.

The EU member-state governments choose the European Commission president, who is then approved by the EP. Member states, in consultation with the incoming president, nominate the other European Commission members, who must also be approved by the EP. The commission is appointed for a five-year term, but can be dismissed by the EP. Many members of its staff work in Brussels, Belgium.

COURT OF JUSTICE

Headquartered in Luxembourg, the Court of Justice of the European Communities consists of one independent judge from each EU country. This court ensures that the common rules decided in the EU are understood and followed uniformly by all the members. The Court of Justice settles disputes over how EU treaties and legislation are interpreted. If national courts are in doubt about how to apply EU rules, they must ask the Court of Justice. Individuals can also bring proceedings against EU institutions before the court.

COURT OF AUDITORS

EU funds must be used legally, economically, and for their intended purpose. The Court of Auditors, an independent EU institution located in Luxembourg, is responsible for overseeing how EU money is spent. In effect, these auditors help European taxpayers get better value for the money that has been channeled into the EU.

OTHER IMPORTANT BODIES

1. European Economic and Social Committee: expresses the opinions of organized civil society on economic and social issues

2. Committee of the Regions: expresses the opinions of regional and local authorities

3. European Central Bank: responsible for monetary policy and managing the euro

4. European Ombudsman: deals with citizens' complaints about mismanagement by any EU institution or body

5. European Investment Bank: helps achieve EU objectives by financing investment projects

Together with a number of agencies and other bodies completing the system, the EU's institutions have made it the most powerful organization in the world.

EU Member States

In order to become a member of the EU, a country must have a stable democracy that guarantees the rule of law, human rights, and protection of minorities. It must also have a functioning market economy as well as a civil service capable of applying and managing EU laws.

The EU provides substantial financial assistance and advice to help candidate countries prepare themselves for membership. As of October 2004, the EU has twenty-five member states. Bulgaria and Romania are likely to join in 2007, which would bring the EU's total population to nearly 500 million.

In December 2004, the EU decided to open negotiations with Turkey on its proposed membership. Turkey's possible entry into the EU has been fraught with controversy. Much of this controversy has centered on Turkey's human rights record and the divided island of Cyprus. If allowed to join the EU, Turkey would be its most-populous member state.

The 2004 expansion was the EU's most ambitious enlargement to date. Never before has the EU embraced so many new countries, grown so much in terms of area and population, or encompassed so many different histories and cultures. As the EU moves forward into the twenty-first century, it will undoubtedly continue to grow in both political and economic strength.

7 FRANCE IN THE EUROPEAN UNION

A founding member of the EU, France has contributed much to the development of this new government.

European Integration

Since the end of imperialism and the dissolving of France's colonial holdings, the country has been in favor of an organization such as the EU—one that unites the various European countries. The reasons for this were varied, but included the fact that, without colonies, France was too small—as were most European nations—to have any international influence. Together, however, these countries could accomplish what was in all of their best interests.

Supranationalism vs. Intergovernmentalism

Since its conception, there have been arguments among member countries in the EU over what approach to government to take. Some agree with intergovernmentalism, or a system in which power is held by member states, and decisions must be reached through a unanimous consensus. Supranationalism, however, gives the power to elected officials. While member states still have power, it is not complete, and decisions are made by majority rule.

France favors intergovernmentalism, as do most larger nations who are nervous about giving over their power and perhaps being forced into a choice that, while good for many of the smaller, less wealthy nations, is not good for them. They also argue that if everything had to be determined unanimously, decisions could take years to reach. The EU has compromised, putting a little of each policy into its government, and has hopefully reached a balance that will work for all the member states.

Arguments with Other Members

Recently, France and Britain have had their disagreements, problems that must be resolved if the EU is to be as successful as possible. Some of these disagreements stem from America's war in Iraq, which Tony Blair, the prime minister of Britain, supported while France did not.

The EU was unable to pass its budget for the years 2007–2013 because of an argument between these two countries. Although there will be another budget vote in the second half of 2005, when Britain has the presidency, neither country is willing to give up certain aspects of its budget.

Another bone of contention is Turkey's proposed membership in the EU. While Britain supports this addition, France believes Turkey should be able to gain full membership, but with only some of the benefits the EU ensures. Hopefully, the two countries will soon find a way to reconcile their differences and work together for the good of the EU.

The EU Constitution

For the first time in the history of the organization, the EU has proposed a constitution. This bill, whose main purpose is to make expansion easier and to downsize the government, needs to be ratified by all member states. France, along with the

Netherlands, voted against the acceptance of the constitution, meaning that the whole organization reached a standstill.

Although French president Jacques Chirac campaigned for the country to accept the new constitution, about 55 percent voted against it. According to Chirac, this creates "a difficult context for the defense of our interests in Europe." If France, one of the largest and most powerful countries in the EU, refuses to ratify this new constitution, it might never happen. Since there was no plan of what to do if this failed, it is possible that the EU will be unable to accept additional members.

France's peaceful countryside

A Calendar of French Festivals

January: January 1 is **New Year's Day**. People celebrate much as they do in the United States, with parties and games. **Epiphany** is January 6. It was on this day that the three kings visited Jesus Christ after his birth. A special cake is made on this day, with a charm or bean in it. Whoever finds the bean in their piece is king or queen for the day.

March/April: Mardi Gras is celebrated as a large festival filled with parades and food. The day after is **Lent**, when people fast and repent their sins in preparation for the Easter season in forty days. On **Good Friday**, the church bells across the country stop ringing. On **Easter (Pâques)**, they are heard again, symbolizing Christ's rising from the dead. Children find Easter eggs hidden around their rooms and yards and in nests previously set out. Games are played with the eggs, including one in which they are tossed up and down; the last one to break the egg is the winner. The children are told that the church bells stopped because they had to make a journey to Rome, where they got the eggs. April 1 is **April Fools' Day**. On this day children stick *Poisson d'Avril*, or paper "April fish," on the backs of as many adults as possible.

May: Labor Day is May 1. While it is a working holiday, it is also a tradition to offer lilies-of-the-valley for good luck. On this day, you don't need a license to sell these flowers, so they are available on almost every corner. **Victory Day (Fête de la Victoire)** is on May 8 and is a time to remember those who died in World War II. It is also a national holiday; schools and businesses are closed. May is also the time of the **Cannes Film Festival**, an annual awards ceremony featuring directors, screenwriters, and actors from all over the world.

June: June 6 is **Mother's Day**. It is celebrated much as in North America, with children giving cards and gifts to their mothers. On this day, moms don't have to work and instead are cared for by their family. The day culminates in a large dinner served in her honor.

July: On **Bastille Day**, which takes place on July 14, the French celebrate the end of the monarchy. It is celebrated with fireworks and military parades. The **Tour de France** is also in July. Cyclists race for three weeks throughout France for the most prestigious cycling award in the world.

August: The **Assumption of the Blessed Virgin Mary** is on August 15. It is a public holiday and celebrates the Catholic belief that Mary did not die, but instead ascended into heaven.

October: While **Halloween** is not a traditional French holiday, it has spread from North America and many French children now go trick-or-treating on October 31. While many customs are the same, the costumes are more likely to be of monsters or ghosts or other scary creatures than of doctors or the other pop-culture figures seen in the United States. Another difference, although it has changed recently, is the fact that many children go door-to-door to stores, rather than people's homes.

November: November 1 is **All Souls' Day**, a time when the French visit the graves of loved ones and reflect on those they have lost. **Armistice Day** is celebrated November 11 and honors those who died in World War I.

December: Christmas (Noël) is December 25. Christmas trees are less popular than in North America, and instead the celebration centers on a crèche. Cakes in the shape of a Yule log are baked and served at a feast after Midnight Mass on Christmas Eve. While French children receive gifts from Père Noël and his companion Pre Fouettard—who reminds Father Christmas whether or not each child was good or bad—adults usually wait until New Year's to exchange presents. In some parts of France, it is le petit Jesus who brings the gifts; in others, Father Nicholas leaves presents in a child's shoe on December 6 and again on Christmas day.

Raspberry Turnovers
(Chaussons aux Framboises)

Ingredients
1 sheet of frozen puff pastry
1 cup of raspberries, plus extra to go on top
1/4 cup raspberry jam
sugar for sprinkling on top

Directions
After defrosting the pastry, unfold it and cut it into 4 equal parts. Put the pieces on a greased baking sheet and refrigerate for 15 minutes. Preheat the oven to 350°F. Mix the jam with the fresh raspberries.

Take the dough out of the refrigerator and put a tablespoon of the berry mixture into a corner of each square. Fold the edges of the pastry over the jam into a triangle. Press the edges together using a fork. Brush the tops with water and sprinkle with sugar. Bake for 15 to 20 minutes, or until golden brown.

Crêpes

Ingredients
3 eggs
1 1/3 cups milk
3/4 cup flour
3/4 teaspoon salt
5 tablespoons melted butter

Directions
Put all the ingredients except the butter in the blender and mix on high for one minute. Strain the batter to remove all lumps. Cover this mixture and keep at room temperature for at least an hour. Or you can refrigerate it for up to a day, as long as it's at room temperature again when you continue.

When ready to prepare, add three tablespoons of the butter, whisking after each addition. Take the foam off what is left of the butter. Heat a skillet to medium heat; you can tell if it's hot enough by sprinkling water on the pan and seeing if it sizzles. After that, brush it with some of the butter. Pour 1/4 cup of the batter into the pan, picking the skillet up and swirling it so the bottom is covered with batter. If there is any extra, pour it back into the bowl. Cook about 20 seconds, or until set. Flip the crêpe over and cook until the other side is light gold.

You can fill the crêpes with almost anything you want—popular fillings in France include jam, ham and cheese, and chocolate.

Croque Monsieurs

This popular sandwich is found in almost every French café.

Ingredients
2 slices of bread
1 tablespoon butter
1 slice of ham
2–3 tablespoons of grated Gruyère cheese

Directions
While preheating a skillet, spread the butter on bother sides of the bread. Make a sandwich out of the ham and cheese and grill as if you were making a grilled cheese sandwich, waiting until one side is golden brown before flipping it over and cooking the other side. For a variation, called a *croque madame*, fry an egg sunny side up and put it on top of the sandwich.

Brie en Croute (Brie in Puffed Pastry)

Serves 8–10

Ingredients
1/2 (17.5 ounce) package frozen puff pastry, thawed
1 8-ounce wheel Brie cheese
1/4 cup sliced walnuts

Directions
Preheat oven to 350°F. Lightly grease a jelly-roll pan or cookie sheet.
Carefully place the puff pastry in the dish. Place the Brie onto the center of the dough. Sprinkle the walnuts evenly over the top. Bring the sides of the dough up to form a bundle around the Brie.
Bake for 15 to 20 minutes. Let cool for 5 minutes before serving with crackers.

Soupe au Fromage (Cheese Soup)

Serves 6

Ingredients
3 ounces salt pork fatback or unsmoked bacon fat
1 large onion, sliced
6 cups vegetable stock
freshly ground pepper
12 ounces mild cheddar cheese
12 ounces rye bread, sliced
2 tablespoons heavy whipping cream

Directions
Preheat oven to 350°F. Render the pork fat in a nonstick skillet. Remove the bacon from the skillet and drain on paper towel. Saute the onion in the fat until brown, being careful not to let it burn.

In a large saucepan, bring the stock to a boil, add the onion, the pork fat, and freshly ground pepper to taste. Crumble the fried bacon and add to the saucepan. Finely grate the cheese onto a plate.

In a 3-quart ovenproof baking dish, alternate layers of bread and the cheese. Sprinkle the top layer with the whipping cream, then pour in the boiling stock. Bake approximately 15 minutes, then serve in warmed bowls.

PROJECT AND REPORT IDEAS

Maps

- Make a map showing the geography and major cities of France.
- Create an export map of France, using a legend to represent all major exports of France.

Reports

- Write a brief report on France's agriculture.
- Write a report on France's concerns within the EU.
- Write a report about France and the Enlightenment.

Biographies
Write a one-page biography on one of the following:

- Charles De Gaulle
- Napoleon Bonaparte
- Marie Antoinette

Journals

- Imagine you are a teenager during World War I or World War II. Write a journal telling about what your life is like.

Projects

- Pretend you are a reporter, and write an article about the storming of the Bastille.
- Make a model of the Eiffel Tower.
- Research Impressionism and make a presentation to the class, showing examples of the artwork.
- Create a painting or sculpture in the Impressionist style.

Group Activities

- Hold a debate, with one side taking the French position on Turkey's acceptance in the EU and the other side taking Britain's side.
- Have a Bastille Day carnival.

CHRONOLOGY

15,000 BCE	The first inhabitants settle in France.
6000 BCE	Agricultural-based cultures settle in France.
700 BCE	Tribes from the north start invading the area.
1 BCE	The Roman Empire attacks what is now France.
100 CE	Christianity begins to spread throughout France.
350–1050	The country suffers a period of decline.
751	Pepin the Short declares himself monarch.
800	Pope Leo crowns Charlemagne head of the Roman Empire.
1152	Henry II, the king of England, the duke of Normandy, marries Eleanor of Aquitaine, making her the first woman to sit on the thrones of two countries: England and France.
1517	Martin Luther begins an attempt to reform the Catholic Church.
1540s	Many Protestants and suspected Protestants are tried and either put to death or sentenced to spend the rest of their lives rowing the galleys.
1598	Henry IV issues the Edict of Nantes.
July 14, 1789	Parisians attack the Bastille.
1789	The Declaration of the Rights of Man and of the Citizen is written.
1793	The king is tried and put to death.
1793	Maximillian Robespierre and his following of radical Jacobeans take over the parliament and the Reign of Terror begins.
1799	Napoleon and his troops attack the government and replace it with the Consulate.
1814	Napoleon abdicates his throne and is exiled.
1815	Napoleon returns to France and is defeated at the Battle of Waterloo.
1821	Napoleon dies in exile.
1905	Church and state are officially separated.
1914	France enters World War I.
1918	France signs an armistice saying that they would demobilize their armed forces.
1928	France joins the League of Nations.
1940	Hitler attacks France.
1944	Allied troops liberate France.
1982	President François Mitterrand attempts to nationalize most of the economy.
1991	France becomes a founding member of the EU.

FURTHER READING/INTERNET RESOURCES

Lotz, Nancy, and Carlene Phillips. *Marie Antoinette and the Decline of French Monarchy.* Greensboro, N.C.: Morgan Reynolds, 2004.

Martin, Judy. *Impressionism.* Templeton, Calif.: Steck-Vaughn, 1995.

Roberts, Lisa. *France.* Philadelphia, Pa.: Chelsea House, 2003.

Sypeck, Jeff. *Holy Roman Empire and Charlemagne in World History.* Berkeley Heights, N.J., Enslow, 2002.

Travel Information

travel-guides.com/data/fra/fra.asp

www.franceway.com

History and Geography

www.bnf.fr/enluminures/themes/t_1/ast_1_04.htm

www.cia.gov/cia/publications/factbook/fields/2113.html

www.uncg.edu/rom/courses/dafein/civ/timeline.htm

Culture and Festivals

www.franceway.com/culture/culture2.htm

www.lonelyplanet.com/destinations/europe/france/culture.htm

Economic and Political Information

www.insee.fr/en/home/home_page.asp

www.nationmaster.com/encyclopedia/Politics-of-France

FOR MORE INFORMATION

Embassy of France
4101 Reservoir Rd. NW
Washington, DC 20007
Tel.: 202-944-6000
e-mail: info@unbafrance-us.org

Embassy of the United States
2 Avenue Gabriel
75382 Paris Cedex 08
Tel.: 33-1-431-22-222

French Mission to the United Nations
245 East 47th Street
New York, NY 10017
Tel.: 212-308-5700
e-mail: france@un.int

U.S. Department of State
2201 C Street NW
Washington, DC 20520
Tel.: 202-642-4000

ally: A person, group, or state joined in association with another.

appeasement: The political strategy of pacifying a potentially hostile nation in the hope of avoiding war.

armistice: A truce in a war to discuss peace terms.

assimilate: To integrate someone into a larger group so that differences are minimized or eliminated.

autonomous: Politically independent and self-governing.

bicameral: Having two separate legislative houses.

blocs: United groups of countries.

capital: Wealth in the form of property or money.

Celts: Early Indo-European people who were spread over much of Europe from the second millennium to the first century BCE.

coniferous: Characteristic of a tree that has thin, needlelike leaves and produces cones.

continental: Characteristic of the continent of Europe.

deciduous: Descriptive term for trees and shrubs that lose their leaves in the fall.

dialect: A regional variation of a language.

Druids: Priests in an ancient religion practiced in Britain, Ireland, and Gaul until the people of those areas were converted to Christianity.

edict: A formal proclamation.

electoral college: A body of electors who officially elect the president and vice president of the United States.

excise: A government-imposed tax on domestic goods.

genocide: The systematic killing, or an attempt to do so, of all the people of a particular national, ethnic, or religious group.

gross domestic product (GDP): The total value of all goods and services produced within a country within a year, minus net income from investments in other countries.

humanist: Someone committed to improving the lives of other people.

hunter-gatherers: Members of a society in which people live by hunting and gathering only, with no crops or livestock raised for food.

indigenous: Native to the area.

Jacobeans: Supporters of King James I.

literacy: The ability to read and write on a functional level.

nationalize: To transfer a business or property from private to government control.

precedent: An action or decision that can be used as an example for future decisions.

ratified: Officially approved.

reparations: Compensation demanded from a defeated nation by the victor in a war.

service sector: The business segment that offers services rather than products.

solidarity: Standing together in a show of unity.

stagnancy: A period of inactivity.

tariff: A government-imposed tax on imports.

unicameral: Having one legislative house.

INDEX

Picture Credits

All photos were taken by Harding House photographer Benjamin Stewart with the exception of the following images:

Used with the permission of the European Communities: pp. 56–57, 59, 62, 65, 66

Photos.com: pp. 60, 68

BIOGRAPHIES

AUTHOR

Jeanine Sanna lives in upstate New York with a variety of animals. In addition to being an author and journalist, she has spent several weeks in France with her French relatives. Jeanine also enjoys traveling, music, and theater.

SERIES CONSULTANTS

Ambassador John Bruton served as Irish Prime Minister from 1994 until 1997. As prime minister, he helped turn Ireland's economy into one of the fastest-growing in the world. He was also involved in the Northern Ireland Peace Process, which led to the 1998 Good Friday Agreement. During his tenure as Ireland's prime minister, he also presided over the European Union presidency in 1996 and helped finalize the Stability and Growth Pact, which governs management of the euro. Before being named the European Commission Head of Delegation in the United States, he was a member of the convention that drafted the European Constitution, signed October 29, 2004.

The European Commission Delegation to the United States represents the interests of the European Union as a whole, much as ambassadors represent their countries' interests to the U.S. government. Matters coming under European Commission authority are negotiated between the commission and the U.S. administration.

Discovering
Cultures

Spain

Lewis K. Parker

BENCHMARK BOOKS

MARSHALL CAVENDISH
NEW YORK

This book is dedicated to all my family members, especially my grandchildren—L.K.P.

With thanks to Sandra Alboum, Alboum & Associates Language Services, for the careful review of this manuscript.

Benchmark Books
Marshall Cavendish
99 White Plains Road
Tarrytown, New York 10591-9001
www.marshallcavendish.com

Text copyright © 2003 by Marshall Cavendish Corporation
Map and illustrations copyright © 2003 by Marshall Cavendish Corporation

All Internet sites were available and accurate when sent to press.

Library of Congress Cataloging-in-Publication Data

Parker, Lewis K.
Spain / by Lewis K. Parker.
p. cm. — (Discovering cultures)
Summary: An introduction to Spain, highlighting the country's geography, people, foods, schools, recreation, celebrations, and language.
Includes bibliographical references and index.
ISBN 0-7614-1520-3
1. Spain—Juvenile literature. [1. Spain.] I. Title. II. Series.
DP17 .P37 2003
946—dc21   2002015301

Photo Research by Candlepants Incorporated
Cover Photo: Richard T. Nowitz/Corbis

The photographs in this book are used by permission and through the courtesy of; *Corbis*: Macduff Everton, 1; Dave G. Houser, 6,13; Nigel Frankis, 8; Michael Busselle, 9, 18; Jon Hicks, 10; Roger Tidman, 11; Richard Bickel, 12; Peter M. Wilson, 14; Alexander Burkatowski, 15; Stephanie Colasanti, 16; Ted Streshinsky, 17, back cover; Nik Wheeler, 19; Charles & Josette Lenars, 20-21; Owen Franken, 22, 33 (left & right); S. Carmona, 30-31, 45; Carl & Pat Purcell, 32; Pablo Corral Vega, 34; Vittoriano Rastelli, 36, 37; Patrick Ward, 38; Pablo San Juan, 39; Marco Cristofori, 40; Bettmann, 44 (top); Archivo Iconographico, 44 (lower). *Grant V. Faint/The Image Bank/Getty Images*: 4-5. *HIRB/Index Stock*: (#556905), 24, (#557318), 25, (#557306), 26, (#557799), 27. *Sofia Moro/Cover/The Image Works*: 28.

Map and illustrations by Salvatore Murdocca
Book design by Virginia Pope

Cover: *The Prado Museum and fountain*; Title page: *A young Spanish girl*

Printed in Hong Kong
1 3 5 6 4 2

Turn the Pages...

¡Bienvenido!

Visitors to Spain receive this friendly greeting. It means "welcome" in Spanish. Spaniards are happy to share their country's white beaches, snowcapped mountains, and seaside villages. It is no wonder that visitors feel welcome.

Young flamenco dancers in traditional dresses

Where in the World Is Spain?

Spain is located in southwestern Europe. It is almost twice the size of the state of Oregon. Spain takes up most of the Iberian Peninsula. It shares the peninsula with Portugal to the west. France lies to the northeast.

The Mediterranean Sea borders Spain's southern and eastern coasts. The Atlantic Ocean is to the south-west and northwest. Spain controls the Canary Islands in the Atlantic. The Balearic Islands in the Mediterranean Sea and some cities on the north coast of Africa are also part of Spain.

Right in the middle of Spain is the Meseta. This high plateau of plains is about half the size of Spain. The Ebro and the Guadal-quivir Rivers flow along the sides of the Meseta.

A Roman bridge across the Guadalquivir River

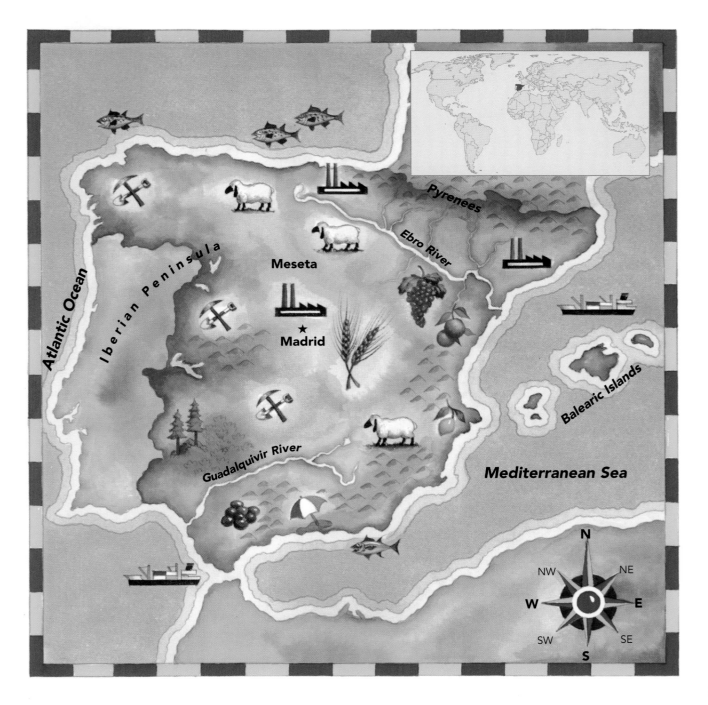

Atlantic Ocean

Iberian Peninsula

Pyrenees

Ebro River

Meseta

★ Madrid

Guadalquivir River

Mediterranean Sea

Balearic Islands

N
NW   NE
W   E
SW   SE
S

A busy street in Madrid

Mountains surround the high flat land. Madrid, the capital city, is located on the Meseta. About five million people live in this modern city of skyscrapers, apartment buildings, and factories. Many of Madrid's factories produce cloth, computers, and cars. Several businesses have their main offices in Madrid.

The Meseta is almost a desert. The high mountains keep winds from blowing rain clouds over the plateau. Summers are very hot and winters can be extremely cold. Except for Madrid, not many people live on the Meseta.

The snowcapped Pyrenees are north of the Meseta. These mountains divide Spain from the rest of Europe. Because northern Spain is close to the ocean, the

The snowy Pyrenees rise above a green valley.

summers are cool and the winters are mild. It rains more here than on the Meseta. There are thick forests inland and beautiful beaches along the coast.

Most Spaniards live in northern Spain. The north is known for its iron mines, steel factories, and fishing grounds. Clothing and shoes are also produced in this area.

Sunbathers on a crowded beach

The eastern coast of Spain faces the Mediterranean Sea. It attracts tourists because of its bright sunshine and gleaming white beaches. The summers are dry and the winters are warm. Because most of the rain falls during the winter, farmers plant their crops in the winter and harvest them in the early summer. This is also a good area for raising sheep. As the weather becomes dry and hot in the summer, shepherds move their herds farther north to cooler areas.

Plains line the eastern Mediterranean coast. The land is very flat and fertile. Farmers produce lemons, limes, oranges, wheat, bananas, dates, wine grapes, sugarcane, and rice. They irrigate their crops from nearby rivers.

Farther south the land is much drier and hotter. Farmers tend olive trees and vineyards. Mining for iron ore, lead, and copper also takes place in the south.

From snowy mountains to sunny coastal plains—Spain has a great variety of landforms and climates!

The Great Bustard

Spain's most unusual bird is the great bustard. It is called a "goose with eagle's wings." It has a body like a goose, but when it flies it opens its great wings and sails like an eagle. This rare bird makes its home on the plains of the Meseta. Weighing about 30 pounds (15 kilograms), the bustard stands on long legs. It has striped black and reddish-brown feathers and a tail that spreads like a fan. The bustard's white moustache sticks out from the sides of its head. Its head looks like the head of a pheasant, but it does not sound like a pheasant. The bustard barks like a dog!

What Makes Spain Spanish?

Spain is made up of several kinds of people. Many Spaniards have ancestors who came to the Iberian Peninsula hundreds of years ago from other parts of Europe. Some came from Ireland and Scotland. Others came from Greece, Italy, and Germany. Invaders from Africa and the Middle East also came to the peninsula. Most Spaniards are a mixture of these groups. A few people can trace their families to the Gypsies that arrived from Hungary.

Spain's official name is the Kingdom of Spain. The people call their country España. Spain's government is a constitutional monarchy. That means the country has a king and a queen who inherit their titles. But the people also elect a president and other members of the government.

People come to Spain from many nations.

Spain is divided into regions, which are like states in the United States. Spanish is the national language. People in some regions speak their ancestors' language in addition to Spanish. Those who live in the northeast corner of the country and along the Mediterranean coast speak Catalan. Signs are written in Catalan and Spanish. Along the Pyrenees Mountains, the Basque people speak Euskara. In Galicia, a region of northwest Spain, a language called Gallego is spoken and taught in schools.

Many people also follow customs handed down from their ancestors. Galicia was settled by people from Ireland and Scotland. Musicians from Galicia play bagpipes as their ancestors once did. In the rural western area, shepherds tend flocks of sheep as their families have done for hundreds of years.

Playing a Galician bagpipe

Outside the Prado Museum

Spain has given the world many things. Flamenco, a kind of singing and dancing, comes from Spain. Many foods such as *gazpacho* (cold tomato soup) and the *tortilla española* (potato omelet) are Spanish creations. People all over the world enjoy Spanish wines. Many wonderful poems, folktales, and stories, such as the story of Don Quixote, also come from Spain. The Prado Museum in Madrid and other museums around the world display the work of great Spanish artists, such as Pablo Picasso and Francisco de Goya.

The Two Saltimbanques *painted by Pablo Picasso*

*A Catholic church
by the Ebro River*

Spain was among the first European countries to explore and colonize North America. Spanish explorers brought the Catholic religion and the Spanish language to the continent. The oldest permanent European town in the United States is Saint Augustine, Florida. It was founded by the Spanish in 1565. In 1598, Spanish missionaries began to settle among the Native American towns along the Rio Grande in what is now the state of New Mexico. Many names of mountains, rivers, and cities in the United States are Spanish. Spanish-style stucco houses with tiled roofs are found throughout the country. You may even live in one!

Traditional Clothing

For festivals, people who live in different regions of Spain wear their traditional clothing. In Andalucía, flamenco dancers usually wear long colorful dresses with ruffles all around the skirt. They stamp their feet as they whirl in these dresses. In Valencia, women may wear long silk dresses with white lace shawls across their shoulders. They wear combs or flowers in their hair. Traditional clothes for Valencian men include short dark jackets and large-brimmed black hats. In Galicia, bagpipe players often wear tall black caps. Basque shepherds may wear a shirt covered with a vest, dark pants, and sandals with socks.

Living in Spain

Not long ago Spain was a nation of small villages. Farmers lived in white houses near the center of the villages. Inside, their houses were often decorated with lovely tiles. Behind the houses were patios where people could sit and talk in the evening shade. They grew crops and raised animals just outside the village. They knew their neighbors, who were usually friends and relatives.

A Spanish farmhouse

Clothes dry on the balcony of an apartment building.

Some people still live in small villages, but only a few are farmers. Now most people live in cities and towns such as Madrid and Barcelona. Their homes are apartments or large, modern houses. They work in office buildings, factories, or shops in the cities.

There are grocery stores in Spain, just as in the United States. However, people also shop at *mercados* (markets). A *mercado* usually has several stalls where customers can buy fresh fruits and vegetables. Some *mercados* sell only one kind of food. A *carnecería* (butcher shop) sells meat while a *panadería* (bakery) sells bread. People usually shop every day for their meals.

Many Spanish people like to eat at restaurants. They enjoy sharing drinks and talking with their friends. Most restaurants and clubs serve *tapas*, tasty snacks made of foods such as olives, mussels, or sausage. *Chorizo* is a *tapa* made of sausage flavored with garlic and paprika. It is usually eaten cold, but can be fried and eaten warm. Another *tapa* is *calamares fritos* (fried squid).

Filling a fruit stand at the mercado

Tapas *in a Spanish restaurant*

Throughout Spain, family life is important. Family members enjoy eating together. *Desayuno*, or breakfast, is the first meal of the day. This is usually a light meal of coffee and a roll or pastry. The coffee is called *café con leche* (coffee with milk).

The midday meal is *almuerzo* (lunch). Taking place between one and three in the afternoon, this is the largest meal of the day. People enjoy the meal, eating slowly while several dishes are served. After a meal, family members may take a *siesta* (short nap) before returning to school or work. Between nine and eleven o'clock, the family eats the last meal of the day. It is called *cena* (supper). This light meal may include Spain's most popular cheese, *queso manchego* (sheep's cheese). It is often served on bread. Families may also serve *gazpacho*, which is made of tomatoes, oil, green peppers, garlic, vinegar, and seasoning.

Let's Eat!
Tortilla Española (Potato Omelet)

This delicious food is served throughout Spain. Ask an adult to help you prepare the following recipe.

Ingredients:

1/2 pound baking potatoes, peeled and sliced

salt

1/2 medium onion, sliced

3 tablespoons olive oil

4 large eggs

Wash your hands. Preheat the oven to 350 degrees Fahrenheit (177 degrees Celsius). Grease a 13 x 9-inch roasting pan with olive oil. Place a layer of potatoes in the pan. Sprinkle salt over the layer. Place half of the onion on the potatoes. Drizzle half of the olive oil over the potatoes. Add another layer of potatoes and repeat with the rest of the onion and olive oil. Roast the potatoes for 45 minutes. Allow to cool.

In a large bowl, beat the eggs with a fork. Add the roasted potato and onion mixture. Press the mixture down so that it is covered with egg. Let sit for about ten minutes.

Heat 1 tablespoon olive oil in a skillet. Quickly add the egg-potato mixture. Flatten the mixture with a spatula and turn the heat down to medium-high. When the underside of the omelet begins to brown, flip.

Use the spatula to smooth out any rough edges. Brown the omelet lightly and turn it again. Cook until the egg is just set.

Slice the omelet in wedges and serve hot to eight people as a *tapa*, or snack.

School Days

All Spanish children between the ages of six and sixteen must attend school. They go to *escuela primaria* (primary school) for six years. But Spain has so many children that all of them cannot go to public school. About one out of every three children attends *escuela privada* (private school), usually run by Catholic churches. The government pays money to these schools to help them teach children. School in Spain is free, but families have to buy books and supplies.

Going to school

Schoolgirls in uniform

Students who go to public schools usually wear T-shirts, jeans, and sneakers. But students who go to private schools wear uniforms. Girls wear white blouses and dark skirts. Boys wear white shirts and dark pants. When the weather gets a little cool, they put on dark jackets.

Children study several subjects such as math, science, and Spanish. Most schools do not have after-school activities such as sports, drama, or band. If children want to play a sport, they have to join a local club. But in some schools, parents have set up sports teams that play after school.

Taking a field trip

The Spanish school year begins in September and ends in June. It is broken into three parts of about eleven weeks each. Children go to school five days a week. School starts at 9 A.M. and usually ends about 6 P.M. Students take a lunch break that often lasts an hour and a half to two hours, so they can go home for lunch. Some schools are skipping the long lunch and closing at 4 P.M. instead. During *fiestas* (festivals), school hours change so children can take time off to celebrate.

Children have long school holidays. They usually get three months off during the summer. For Christmas they have two weeks vacation. They have another week off for Easter. During these times, many families travel or ski.

Students gather in front of a bulletin board.

After leaving *escuela primaria*, children attend *escuela secundaria* (secondary school). This is like a high school where they remain for four years. Classes in *escuela secundaria* may include English, Spanish history, and religion.

When students complete *escuela secundaria*, they can choose to attend *bachillerato* (college prep school) or a trade school for two years. In *bachillerato*, the students prepare for studies at a university. Students in the trade school learn skills that will help them find jobs.

Working on the computer

Students who earn good grades usually go on to a university to study for a certain career. They may become doctors or teachers. Students do not live at the university. They only go to school to take classes and tests.

The people of Spain take education very seriously. They realize that the future of their country lies with their students. For Spanish children, education provides the gateway to the future and the opportunity for success.

Pelota Pared
(Wall Ball)

Pelota pared is a popular game that children play during their breaks at school. Children use the wall of a building, a tennis ball, and chalk to play. First, a horizontal line is drawn on the wall with the chalk. The line is about three feet from the ground. Every player has a number. Player one bounces the ball on the floor and hits it with one hand. As the ball strikes the wall, the player calls out another number. The player with that number must hit the ball before it bounces twice on the ground. Then, that player calls out a number to continue the game. A player is out if he cannot hit the ball before the second bounce or if the ball hits the wall under the line. The last player left is the winner.

Just for Fun

When children are not in school, there are many things to keep them busy. Children who live in villages often do chores on their families' farms. They help grow fruits and vegetables like olives, grapes, melons, or peaches.

Many children enjoy going to the movies. Others watch television or play video games. Families may also go to the many amusement parks. Trips to wild animal reserves, science museums, and planetariums are also popular.

Because the weather is generally warm throughout Spain, most children play outside. After-school activities may include riding bikes, flying kites, fishing, or playing a sport.

Many children play on basketball teams. There are courts in most city parks. Other children play *fútbol* (soccer). This is the most popular sport in

Soccer fans celebrate a victory.

Two cyclists stop for a drink.

Spain. Hometown soccer teams are found everywhere. Large stadiums in Madrid and Barcelona attract thousands of people to cheer for their favorite professional teams like Real Madrid or Barça.

Another popular sport is bicycling. Road races are held in many towns and villages. Riders come from all over the world to compete in the Vuelta a España (Tour of Spain), a famous bicycle race.

Pelota is also popular. This game is called the fastest sport of all. Families can see *pelota* games in stadiums. Pro players hold curved baskets called *cestas*. They use the *cestas* to hurl a hard ball against a wall. Opponents must catch the speeding ball in their own *cestas* and throw it back. The ball may travel almost 200 miles (322 kilometers) per hour.

Pelota *players use a* cesta *to throw the ball.*

Children and their families may enjoy mountain climbing, hiking, and skiing in the Pyrenees. Skiing also takes place in the Cantabrian Mountains and in the Sierra Nevada. Spain also has many fine beaches. Families often spend their free time on the coast, swimming or waterskiing.

Children play at the beach.

Bullfighting

Bullfighting is popular in Spain. Major cities have large bullrings where thousands of people watch the bullfights, usually on Sundays from March to October.

The bullfight begins with a parade in the bullring. After the parade, a bull is sent into the ring. A fighting bull is large and strong. Then the matador enters. He or she is dressed in a formal and highly decorated costume. The tight pants are embroidered in gold and silver and reach to the matador's calf. A short jacket the same color as the pants and also richly embroidered covers the shirt. A two-cornered black hat, pink stockings, and black slippers complete the traditional costume.

During the bullfight, the matador faces the bull alone. The matador waves a red cape. The angry bull charges. The matador moves gracefully out of the way, coming as close as possible to the bull's horns without getting hurt.

35

Let's Celebrate!

It seems that every day in Spain is a day of celebration. A fiesta may be held for one day of the week or it may continue for a whole week, giving people the chance to dress up and enjoy themselves.

Spain is a Catholic country and religion is very important to the people. Many feast days are held to celebrate saints. And almost every village has a special day to honor its patron saint with floats, fireworks, parades, and dancing.

Carnaval (Carnival) is usually held in February or March, about forty days before Easter. Carnaval is a time to have fun. People enjoy lots of games, food, and dancing. Bands of musicians called *chirigotas* play their guitars on the streets. The biggest celebration is

A Carnaval clown

Dressed for Carnaval in Cadiz

held in Cadiz. People wearing unusual costumes and masks wander the streets singing playful songs.

The week before Easter is called Semana Santa (Holy Week). In every town and city, parades are held from the local churches to the large cathedrals and back again. The parades usually feature colorful floats showing scenes from the life of

Crowds watch a Holy Week procession.

Queens of the April fair

Jesus. Bells are rung in many towns. In some cities, mass is celebrated with orchestras and choirs.

Crowds come to the city of Seville for Feria de Abril (April fair). This festival is held every April, two weeks after Easter. It goes on for six days and nights and ends with fireworks. More than a thousand booths are set up on the fairground where delicious foods and crafts such as handmade lace are sold. Women in colorful long dresses parade on beautiful horses and carriages through the fairgrounds. At the end of May, the *fiesta* of Corpus Christi reminds Catholics of their faith. In some places, parades are held on carpets made of flowers.

In December, Spain celebrates Navidad (Christmas). Families sing Christmas carols and usually put up nativity sets instead of Christmas trees. On Christmas Eve, many families have dinner together and attend midnight mass. Most families do not exchange gifts until January 6. This is called the Feast of the Epiphany, or Three Kings Day. This day honors the three kings who traveled long distances to bring gifts to the baby Jesus. Many towns hold Epiphany parades

Christmas in Madrid

and actors dressed as the Three Kings arrive on camels or horses or in helicopters to pass out gifts.

On New Year's Eve, people follow a tradition of eating twelve grapes at exactly midnight when the clocks chime twelve times. They have to eat twelve grapes in twelve seconds! If they can do that, they believe they will have good luck the next year. Spanish fiestas feature all kinds of different traditions. In some areas, people participate in contests in which oxen pull heavy loads. Others race boats on the rivers. In one city, people celebrate *La Tomatina* by throwing tomatoes at one another!

Fallas de San José

A traditional *fiesta* is held every year in Valencia. It is called the Fallas de San José (Bonfires of Saint Joseph). The festival honors San José (Saint Joseph), the patron saint of carpenters. For the festival children and their families make hundreds of papier-mâché *gigantes* (giants). For a week they are placed in the middle of the city for everyone to see. On March 19 fireworks are placed inside the figures. One by one, the figures are set on fire. The explosions make a terrific noise, and by midnight the city glows orange from the flames.

The Spanish flag features three horizontal bands of red (top), yellow (center), and red (bottom). The national coat of arms lies on the yellow band. At the middle of the coat of arms is the royal seal. On each side of the seal are the Pillars of Hercules, which represent the Rock of Gibraltar (Europe) and Ceuta (Africa). These are two high points of land on each side of the Strait of Gibraltar.

Spain is a member of the European Union (EU). In January 2002, Spain and eleven other states within the EU began to use the same currency, or money. This currency is called the Euro. Euro coins share common European designs on the front, but the designs on the back of the coins change from nation to nation. Euro banknotes, or paper money, are the same in all twelve nations.

Count in Spanish

English	Spanish	Say it like this:
one	uno	OO-noh
two	dos	DOHS
three	tres	TREHS
four	cuatro	KWA-troh
five	cinco	THEEN-koh
six	seis	SAYS
seven	siete	see-EH-teh
eight	ocho	OH-choh
nine	nueve	NWEH-veh
ten	diez	dee-EHTH

Glossary

España (es-PAHN-yah) Spanish name for Spain.

flamenco (flah-MEN-coh) Type of Spanish dance and music.

matador (mah-tah-DOR) Person who fights a bull in a bullfight.

mercado (mehr-CAH-doh) Market in a Spanish suburb or village.

patron saint Saint who looks over a particular country or group of people.

peninsula Body of land surrounded on three sides by water.

plateau Raised flat area of land.

Pyrenees High mountains that border Spain and France.

tapa (TAH-pah) Snack food usually eaten in the afternoon or evening.

tortilla (tor-TEE-yah) An omelet, often with potatoes.

Proud to Be Spanish

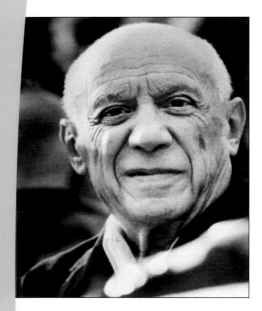

Pablo Picasso (1881–1973)

Pablo Picasso is considered one of Spain's greatest artists. Born in Málaga, he moved to Paris, France, when he was a young man. There he worked as an artist. Picasso made many paintings in a style of art called Cubism. These paintings are not realistic. Instead, the art looks like geometric shapes. Picasso was also a sculptor. One of Picasso's greatest works is a large painting called *Guernica*. In this painting, Picasso showed the terrible destruction that occurs during war. *Guernica* is displayed at the Reina Sofía National Museum in Madrid.

Miguel de Cervantes Saavedra (1547–1616)

Miguel de Cervantes Saavedra was born in Alcalá de Henares, a small town east of Madrid. He is considered one of Spain's greatest writers. Cervantes is best known as the author of the comical book, *Don Quixote de la Mancha* (Don Quixote of La Mancha). In this book a country gentleman thinks that he is a knight and gets into all kinds of funny adventures. At one point, Don Quixote jousts with a windmill! Cervantes based much of the book on his own life. He joined the army when he was twenty-three. In 1575, pirates captured him and kept him a prisoner in Africa. He remained there for five years until his family had collected enough money to buy his freedom. Back in Spain, Cervantes worked for the government. In 1605, he published *Don Quixote de La Mancha*, which became a great success. In 1965, Cervantes's book was turned into a musical, *Man of La Mancha*.

Arantxa Sánchez-Vicario (1971–   )

Arantxa Sánchez-Vicario, nicknamed the "Barcelona Bumblebee," is considered the top female tennis player in Spain and one of the best in the world. She was born on December 18, 1971, in Barcelona. She started playing tennis at the age of four. Sánchez-Vicario became so attached to her tennis racket that she had a chair for it at the family dinner table. Since turning pro in 1986, she has won a long list of tournaments against some of the world's best tennis players. In 1994, she was named the International Tennis Federation's world champion. Four years later, she received Spain's highest award, the Príncipe de Asturias (Prince of Asturias Award), for her achievements in tennis. Arantxa Sánchez-Vicario is the first Spanish woman to receive this honor.

Find Out More

Books

Spain by Kathleen W. Deady. Bridgestone Books, Minnesota, 2001.

Spain by Henry Arthur Pluckrose. Franklin Watts, New York, 1998.

Spain: the Culture by Noa Lior and Tara Steele. Crabtree Publishing Co., New York, 2002.

A Taste of Spain by Bob Goodwin and Candi Perez. Thomson Learning, New York, 1995.

Welcome to Spain by Geraldine Mesenas. Gareth Stevens Publishing, Wisconsin, 2000.

Web sites

The Prado Museum **http://museoprado.mcu.es** provides an excellent tour of the museum.

For links to photographs and maps of Spain, plus numerous sites on the country's culture and history, go to **http://www.yahooligans.com/around_the_world/countries/spain/**.

Video

Questar's *Video Visits Travel Collection: Discovering Spain* provides a tour of Spain that includes a look at the culture of the cities and the countryside.

Index

Page numbers for illustrations are in **boldface.**

About the Author

Lewis K. Parker has worked as a teacher, editor, and writer. He is the author of many articles, plays, and books for young readers. He enjoys traveling and writing about various countries.